W9-CNA-362

Sports in America
2000–2009

JIM GIGLIOTTI
AND JOHN WALTERS

SERIES FOREWORD BY
LARRY KEITH

CHELSEA HOUSE
PUBLISHERS
An imprint of Infobase Publishing

2000–2009
Sports in America

Chelsea House
An imprint of Infobase Publishing
132 West 31st Street
New York NY 10001

Library of Congress Cataloging-in-Publication Data

Gigliotti, Jim.
  Sports in America, 2000-2009 / by Jim Gigliotti and John Walters ; foreword by Larry Keith.
      p. cm. — (Sports in America)
  Includes bibliographical references and index.
  ISBN-13: 978-1-60413-457-5 (hardcover : alk. paper)
  ISBN-10: 1-60413-457-7 (hardcover : alk. paper) 1. Sports—United States—History—21st century. I. Walters, John (John Andrew) II. Title. III. Series.

  GV583.G545 2010
  796.097309'05—dc22

                              2010011084

Chelsea House books are available at special discounts when purchased in bulk quantities for businesses, associations, institutions, or sales promotions. Please call our Special Sales Department in New York at (212) 967-8800 or (800) 322-8755.

You can find Chelsea House on the World Wide Web at http://www.chelseahouse.com

Produced by the Shoreline Publishing Group LLC
President/Editorial Director: James Buckley Jr.
Contributing Editor: Jim Gigliotti
Text design by Thomas Carling, carlingdesign.com
Index by Nanette Cardon, IRIS

Photo credits: AP/Wide World: 7, 9, 10, 12, 13, 14, 21, 22, 28, 29, 30, 31, 33, 36, 37, 38, 39, 42, 44, 46, 49, 50, 54, 55, 56–57, 63, 66, 69, 71, 76, 80, 81, 86; Getty Images: 3, 15, 16–17, 18, 23, 25, 26, 35, 41, 45, 52, 53, 58, 61, 62, 65, 72, 73, 75, 78, 79, 83, 84, 88, 89.
Sports icons by Bob Eckstein.

Cover printed by Bang Printing, Brainerd, MN
Book printed and bound by Bang Printing, Brainerd, MN
Date printed: July 2010

Printed in the United States of America.

10 9 8 7 6 5 4 3 2 1

This book is printed on acid-free paper.

CONTENTS

Boston Red Sox (page 45)

FEB 1 9 2011

FOREWORD

BY LARRY KEITH

WHEN THE EDITORS OF SPORTS IN AMERICA invited me to write the foreword to this important historical series I recalled my experience in the 1980s as the adjunct professor for a new sports journalism course in the graduate school of Columbia University. Before granting their approval, the faculty at that prestigious Ivy League institution asked, Do sports matter? Are they relevant? Are they more than just fun and games?

The answer—an emphatic yes—is even more appropriate today than it was then. As an integral part of American society, sports provide insights to our history and culture and, for better or worse, help define who we are.

Sports In America is much more than a compilation of names, dates, and facts. Each volume chronicles accomplishments and expansions of the possible. Not just in the physical ability to perform, but in the ability to create goals and determine methods to achieve them. In this way, sports, the sweaty offspring of recreation and competition, resemble any other field of endeavor. I certainly wouldn't equate the race for a gold medal with the race to the moon, but the building blocks are the same: the intelligent application of talent, determination, research, practice, and hard work to a meaningful objective.

Sports matter because they show us in high definition. They communicate examples of determination, courage, and skill. They often embody a heroic human-interest story, overcoming poverty, injustice, injury, or disease. The phrase, "Sports is a microcosm of life," could also read "Life is a microcosm of sport."

Consider racial issues. When Jackie Robinson of the Brooklyn Dodgers broke through major league baseball's "color barrier" in 1947, the significance extended beyond the national pastime. Precisely because baseball was the national pastime, this epochal event reverberated throughout every part of American society.

To be sure, black stars from individual sports had preceded him (notably Joe Louis in boxing and Jesse Owens in track), and others would follow (Arthur Ashe in tennis and Tiger Woods in golf), but Robinson stood out as an important member of a team. He wasn't just playing with the Dodgers, he was traveling with them, living with them. He was a black member of a white athletic family. The benefits of integration could be appreciated far beyond the borough of Brooklyn. In 1997, Major League Baseball retired his "42" jersey number.

Sports have always been a laboratory for social awareness and change. Robinson integrated big league box scores eight years before the U.S. Supreme Court ordered the integration of public schools. The Paralympics (1960) and Special Olympics (1968) easily predate the Americans with Disabilities Act (1990). The mainstreaming of disabled athletes was especially apparent in 2007 when double amputee Jessica Long, 15, won the AAU Sullivan Award as America's top amateur. Women's official debut in the Olympic Games, though limited to swimming, occurred in 1912, seven years before they got the right to vote. So even if these sports were tardy in opening their doors, in another way, they were ahead of their times. And if it was necessary to break down some of those doors—Title IX support for female college athletes comes to mind—so be it. Basketball star Candace Parker won't let anyone keep her from the hoop.

Another area of importance, particularly as it affects young people, is substance abuse. High school, college, and professional teams all oppose the illegal use of drugs, tobacco, and alcohol. In most venues, testing is mandatory, and tolerance is zero. The confirmed use of performance enhancing drugs has damaged the reputations of such superstar athletes as Olympic sprinters Ben Johnson and Marion Jones, cyclist Floyd Landis, and baseball sluggers Manny Ramirez and Alex Rodriguez. Some athletes have lost their careers, or even their lives, to substance abuse. Conversely, other athletes have used their fame to caution young people about submitting to peer pressure or making poor choices.

Fans care about sports and sports personalities because they provide entertainment and self-identify—too often at a loss of priorities. One reason sports have flourished in this country is their support from governmental bodies. When a city council votes to help underwrite the cost of a sports facility or give financial advantages to the owners of a team, it affects the pocketbook of every taxpayer, not to mention the local ecosystem. When high schools and colleges allocate significant resources to athletics, administrators believe they are serving the greater good, but at what cost? Decisions with implications beyond the sports page merit everyone's attention.

In World War II, our country's sporting passion inspired President Franklin Roosevelt to declare that professional games should not be cancelled. He felt the benefits to the national psyche outweighed the risk of gathering large crowds at central locations. In 2001, another generation of Americans also continued to attend large-scale sports events because, to do otherwise, would "let the terrorists win." Being there, being a fan, yelling your lungs out, cheering victory and bemoaning defeat, is a cleansing, even therapeutic exercise. The security check at the gate is just part of the price of stepping inside. Even before there was a 9/11, there was a bloody terrorist assault at the Munich Olympic Games in 1972.

The popular notion "Sports build character" has been better expressed "Sports reveal character." We've witnessed too many coaches and athletes break rules of fair play and good conduct. The convictions of NBA referee Tim Donaghy for gambling and NFL quarterback Michael Vick for operating a dog-fighting ring are startling recent examples. We've even seen violence and cheating in youth sports, often by parents of a (supposed) future superstar. We've watched (at a safe distance) fans "celebrate" championships with destructive behavior. I would argue, however, that these flaws are the exception, not the rule, that the good of sports far outweighs the bad, that many of life's success stories took root on an athletic field.

Any serious examination of sports leads to the question of athletes as standards for conduct. Professional basketball star Charles Barkley created quite a stir in 1993 when he used a Nike shoe commercial to declare, "I am not paid to be a role model." The knee-jerk response argued, "Of course you are, because kids look up to you," but Barkley was right to raise the issue. He was saying that, in making lifestyle choices in language and behavior, young people should look elsewhere for role models, ideally to responsible parents or guardians.

The fact remains, however, that athletes occupy an exalted place in our society, especially when they are magnified in the mass media, sports talk radio, and the blogosphere. The athletes we venerate can be as young as a high school basketball player or as old as a Hall of Famer. (They can even be dead, as Babe Ruth's commercial longevity attests.) They are honored and coddled in a way few mortals are. Regrettably, we can be quick to excuse their excesses and ignore their indulgences. They influence the way we live and think: Ted Williams inspired patriotism as a wartime fighter pilot; Muhammad Ali's opposition to the Vietnam War on religious grounds, validated by the Supreme Court, encouraged the peace movement; Magic Johnson's contraction of the HIV/AIDS virus brought better understanding to a little-understood disease. No wonder we elect them—track stars, football coaches, baseball pitchers—to represent us in Washington. Meanwhile, television networks pay huge sums to sports leagues so their teams can pay fortunes for their services.

Indeed, it has always been this way. If we, as a nation, love sports, then we, quite naturally, will love the men and women who play them best. In return, they provide entertainment, release and inspiration. From the beginning of the 20th century until now, Sports In America is their story-and ours.

Larry Keith is the former Assistant Managing Editor of Sports Illustrated. *He created the editorial concept for* SI Kids *and was the editor of the official Olympic programs in 1996, 2000 and 2002. He is a former adjunct professor of Sports Journalism at Columbia University and is a member of the North Carolina Journalism Hall of Fame.*

INTRODUCTION
2000–2009

The year 2000 saw the beginning of a new year, a new decade, and a new millennium. The entire world held its breath in fear of the "Y2K" problem. That was the worry that computer systems would crash when they suddenly had to read dates that started with 2 instead of 1. As the clocks ticked down to the end of the 1000s, however, other than a few little bugs, Y2K was one crisis that never happened.

If only the rest of the decade had gone so smoothly.

The 2000s ended with *Time* Magazine calling the 10-year span the "decade from hell." Disaster followed disaster around the world, beginning with the sudden, shocking horror of the 9/11/2001 attacks on the United States. A war in Afghanistan began (and continues), followed by a war in Iraq. Hurricane Katrina swamped New Orleans and Gulf Coast Mississippi in 2004, while a series of financial disasters nearly swamped the U.S. economy in the final years of the decade. It was, in short, a rotten way to start a new millennium.

As they had in past decades, people turned their eyes toward America's athletes and teams for entertainment, for relief from the bad news of the "real" world, and for encouragement that things could be brighter.

In sports, they found several inspiring and uplifting individual stories. Cancer survivor Lance Armstrong made the Tour de France his personal showcase. Danica Patrick forged in-roads in the male-dominated world of auto racing. Swimmer Michael Phelps came through with an entire nation pulling for him in the 2008 Olympics.

Team sports thrived, too. Baseball's Boston Red Sox ended a "curse" that spanned the better part of a century. NASCAR sped near the forefront of the American sports consciousness, while pro football stayed there with a couple of classic Super Bowls to close the decade.

Sadly, though, sports weren't immune to the troubles of the 2000s. Perhaps the ambivalence of the decade was best illustrated by its most prominent athlete, Tiger Woods. For almost the entire 10 years, Tiger thrilled fans with incomparable feats on the golf course, including a dramatic U.S. Open for the ages. Suddenly, as the decade came to an end, Tiger made headlines for all the wrong reasons in November of 2009 (see page 88).

Time to Play . . . and Pray *Major League Baseball returned seven days after 9/11, signalling a return to normalcy.*

Other athletes used drugs, cheated, and broke the law in increasing numbers. The massive, unblinking scrutiny of the Internet made it seem even worse than it was, as every tiny twitter of bad news sped around the globe in moments. The amount of money went up and up in sports, leading more people to make more bad choices, while the pressure to excel drove others to cut corners to win.

Still, amid the scandals and arrests, sports did supply more of the events that have cheered Americans for more than a century. In the wake of 9/11, sports venues became national places of remembrance. After Katrina in 2004, the return of sports to New Orleans was seen as a sign of the hard-hit area's rebirth. In the midst of 2008's financial crisis, Olympic glory brought a shine back into people's lives.

As America and the world embark on this new millennium, sports will continue to play a huge part in people's lives, for better or worse.

2000

Two Number Ones

The ongoing controversy about college football's national championship continued—and even grew—as the new millennium began. In 1998, the Bowl Championship Series (BCS) had been created to "fix" the problem of not being able to match up the top two teams at the end of the season in a post-bowl Championship Game. Because all major conferences already had agreements to send their champions to certain bowl games, pitting the number-one team against the number-two team rarely happened. The BCS created a system in which human polls and computers combined to determine the top teams and override the traditional conference tie-ins for a one versus two showdown to determine a true national champion—in theory, anyway.

The biggest impetus for the BCS came in 1997. The University of Michigan Wolverines, ranked number one in both national polls (one voted by coaches, one by writers), won the Rose Bowl on New Year's Day of 1998. But the Nebraska Cornhuskers won the Orange Bowl later that night, and the next day ascended to the top spot in the coaches' poll. Michigan and Nebraska shared the national title. The argument went on for months, with fans and the media crying for clarity. Thus the BCS was born, but its results have been mixed.

In 2000, the BCS computers spit out two top teams: Florida State and Oklahoma. Most fans agreed that undefeated Oklahoma deserved a spot. However, the University of Miami also had only one loss . . . and Miami beat Florida State earlier in the season. Oklahoma ended the controversy by beating Florida State by an unusual 13–2 score. However, the theme of "Who's Number One?" and the issue of just who decides would resonate throughout the decade.

Cinderella Pigskin

Call it coincidence, luck, or a universal leveling of playing fields, but the number of teams winning their first championships as the curtain rose on the new century was unprecedented. Start with the NFL. From Super Bowl XI in 1977, the year the Oakland Raiders won their first NFL title, until Super Bowl XXXII in 1998, when the Denver Broncos at last claimed the Lombardi Trophy, only

He Roared *Tiger Woods destroyed the competition in the U.S. Open, winning by 15 strokes (page 11).*

four teams became first-time champions. Then, following a Broncos' repeat in 1999, came a run of four such teams.

The St. Louis Rams were the first of the four straight first-time Super Bowl winners when they won Super Bowl XXXIV on January 30, 2000. They joined that club in dramatic fashion, capping off one of the best Cinderella stories in recent NFL history.

The Rams' offense became known as "The Greatest Show on Turf" for its high-scoring, pass-happy style. The ringmaster of this football circus was quarterback Kurt Warner, who to everyone's surprise except his own became the league's MVP.

Dream Come True *Strong-armed quarterback Kurt Warner was named the Super Bowl MVP as he led the Rams to a surprising Super Bowl victory. His unlikely journey to the top gained national attention.*

starter Trent Green put Warner in the Rams' starting lineup, and he showed everyone what they'd been missing. His rocket arm and calm in the pocket helped the Rams light up scoreboards and storm to its first NFC title since 1979.

After knocking off the Vikings and Buccaneers in the playoffs, St. Louis faced the Tennessee Titans in what proved to be a very entertaining Super Bowl. The Rams jumped to a 16–0 lead, but the Titans charged back to tie the game. Warner hit it big late, though, with a 73-yard touchdown pass to Isaac Bruce that gave the Rams a 23–16 lead. Then, the Titans' Steve McNair led his team down to the 10-yard line with just six seconds left. On the final play of the game, Rams linebacker Mike Jones tackled Titans receiver Kevin Dyson just one yard shy of the end zone, a play that quickly earned the nickname of "The Tackle." Warner was the game's MVP, capping off his storybook season.

McSorley Pays

Pro hockey has always been a tough sport, with on-ice fighting almost as much a part of the game—and the appeal for fans—as slap shots and great saves. It's a game of action and hard hitting. However, in February, one player went too far. Both he and his victim paid the price.

Marty McSorley of the Boston Bruins smashed Donald Brashear of the Vancouver Canucks with just three seconds left in their game on February 21. Brashear fell to the ice and hit his head quite hard. He suffered a concussion and memory loss, though he later recovered fully. However, McSorley's vicious swing shocked players

Warner had played college football at tiny Northern Iowa and was actually working in a supermarket when he finally got a chance with the indoor Arena Football League's Iowa Barnstormers. NFL teams noticed but still thought he needed seasoning, so he was sent to play in the NFL's Europe League. After starting for the Amsterdam Admirals, Warner's odyssey landed him in St. Louis. An injury to

and fans. He was immediately suspended by the National Hockey League (NHL) for the rest of the season. In October 2000, McSorley was convicted of assault, a very rare penalty for actions taken during a sporting event. He was put on probation by the court in Vancouver. The NHL extended his suspension through February 2001, and McSorley retired, never to play in the NHL again.

Hockey remains a rough and dangerous sport, but the McSorley incident drew new attention to fighting and hitting that went beyond the norm, and the NHL, though still not perfect, has been a much safer league in the years since.

Everyone's Chasing Tiger

Golfer Tiger Woods kept proving why he is the real deal (though by the end of the decade, his life would take a major turn; see page 88). Make that unreal. He continued to dominate the PGA Tour into the new millennium, as his impact on the sport reached the status of baseball giant Babe Ruth. Other gifted golfers, such as Ernie Els, Phil Mickelson, David Duval, Jim Furyk, and Sergio Garcia, mounted valiant challenges, yet Tiger beat them all to remain the top-ranked player in the world. Winning tournaments by ridiculous margins, drawing unprecedented galleries and TV ratings, and lifting his game to ever-loftier levels, Woods gained further consideration as perhaps the best golfer ever.

The year 2000 was perhaps the finest of his amazing career. On June 18 at Pebble Beach, California, he captured his first U.S. Open and third major tournament in record-setting fashion. His 15-stroke victory was the largest winning margin ever in a major. (Near the end of the decade, Hall-of-Fame golfer Tom Watson called it golf's biggest achievement.) Just 35 days later, on July 23, Woods wrapped up a 19-under-par performance on the Old Course at St. Andrews, Scotland—the esteemed birthplace of golf—to clinch the British Open. With that, Tiger, at age 24, became the youngest golfer to have won all four majors; the great Jack Nicklaus was two years older when he achieved his career Grand Slam.

Then, on August 20, down by two strokes to Bob May early in the final round of the PGA Championship at Valhalla Golf Club in Louisville, Kentucky, Tiger birdied the last two holes of regulation to force a three-hole playoff. A birdie and two pars later, he had his third major of the year, a feat last accomplished by Ben Hogan (1912–1997) in 1953. "Someday I'll tell my grandkids I played in the same tournament as Tiger Woods," mar-

Signs of Things to Come

After landing on the Women's Tennis Association (WTA) Tour scene in the late 1990s, the Williams sisters, Serena and Venus, ruled the 2000s, especially in the prestigious Grand Slam events. They kicked off their decade of dominance in 2000. Venus defeated her younger sister in the semifinals at Wimbledon en route to her first Grand Slam title, topping reigning champion Lindsay Davenport. Venus beat Davenport again in the U.S. Open final, then capped off a sensational year with the singles crown at the Summer Olympic Games in Sydney, Australia—where she and Serena also collected the doubles gold medal.

Shaq Attack *Powerful center Shaquille O'Neal dominated the boards and joined high-scoring guard Kobe Bryant to lead the Los Angeles Lakers back to the NBA championship.*

veled Watson (b.1949). "We are witnessing a phenomenon here that the game may never, ever see again."

The Lake Show Returns

In the 1960s and again in the 1980s, the Los Angeles Lakers were among the best teams in the NBA, winning numerous championships. In June of 2000, they returned to the top, winning their first title since 1988. The team was led by one of the most powerful one-two punches in sports: slashing guard Kobe Bryant and high-scoring (and quote-spouting) center Shaquille O'Neal.

The two brought enormous talent to the floor, but also big egos off it. It took the addition of super-coach Phil Jackson to pull them together into champions. Jackson had previously led the Chicago Bulls (and Michael Jordan) to six NBA titles. The Lakers stormed through the regular season, with O'Neal earning league MVP honors. He led the league in field goals and field-goal percentage, a testament to his power of getting close to the hoop. (Being 7 feet 2 inches and 325 pounds was helpful in that regard!) Bryant, meanwhile, gave opponents fits with his clutch outside shooting and blazing speed to the hoop.

The Lakers faced the Indiana Pacers in the NBA Finals. Indiana proved to be little competition, with Los Angeles winning in six games. "Shaq Daddy" was the NBA Finals MVP. A few days later, he and Kobe led a boisterous victory parade through downtown Los Angeles. The championship was the first of three straight for the Lakers, with O'Neal earning MVP honors in the Finals each time.

Sampras Is Number One

In tennis, the four Grand Slam tournaments are the Australian, French, and U.S. Opens, and the Wimbledon Championships in England. Since the first Wimbledon in 1886, no one had won more than 12 Grand Slam titles in a career . . . until 2000. With a victory at Wimbledon in July, American star Pete Sampras captured his 13th career Grand Slam tennis title, passing Roy Emerson for the all-time record.

Sampras was not a flashy player, nor blessed with a stunning off-court personality like so many stars of his era. However, he was a superb player, outstanding at the serve-and-volley game that wins on grass at Wimbledon (he won there seven times) and also able to play the power game on hard courts at the U.S. Open, where he was a five-time winner. He would run his record to 14 Grand Slams with a win at the 2002 U.S. Open before retiring in 2003. In 2009, Swiss star Roger Federer would top Sampras' total, but Sampras remains among the greatest stars in world tennis history.

Despite Tarnish, Summer Olympics Shine

Scandal rocked the Olympic movement in November 1998 when it was alleged that International Olympic Committee (IOC) members had been bribed by Salt Lake City, Utah, officials to influence the city's selection as the site for the 2002 Winter Games. An investigation prompted the resignations of two top Salt Lake Olympic Organizing Committee ex-

The New Boss *The strong and steady play of Pete Sampras dominated the hard and grass courts and helped him break the all-time Grand Slam record.*

ecutives and several IOC members, as well as sweeping reforms throughout the IOC, based in Lausanne, Switzerland. (In early 2004, a Utah judge threw out the case against the U.S. official who was charged, citing lack of evidence. However, the IOC reforms remained in place.)

Many worried that the ongoing scandal would affect the 2000 Summer Olympics set for Sydney, Australia, in September. However, with no Olympic athletes accused in the mess, the focus in Australia was on competition, not controversy. Americans brought home the most medals—36 gold, 24 silver, and 31 bronze—while turning in a number of

Golden Women *Lisa Leslie (facing camera) was the star as the U.S. women's basketball team captured the gold medal at the 2000 Summer Games in Australia.*

United States outshined its Aussie hosts, 14 golds to 5.

Sprinting sensation Marion Jones (b.1975) claimed that she was going to win five gold medals, which would have been an American first for any track athlete. She fell short, but three gold medals and two bronze medals were more than impressive. She and teammate Maurice Greene claimed the title of "World's Fastest Humans" by winning their respective 100-meter races.

The Olympic spirit celebrates underdogs, and there was none more lionized in Sydney than Greco-Roman wrestler Rulon Gardner of the United States. With no major title to his name, the hulking Wyoming native upset legendary Russian Alexander "The Beast" Karelin, who hadn't lost a match in 13 years. Nearly as stunning was the 4–0 upset victory by the American baseball team over the heavily favored Cubans in the championship game.

The Subway Series

In the 1950s, New York City was baseball heaven. Every World Series in the decade except 1959 featured at least one team from the city. In five of those years, two teams from Gotham met up in what were called "Subway Series," after the mode of transportation fans could use to go back and forth to the games. However, the Brooklyn Dodgers and New York Giants moved to the West Coast in 1958. The New York Mets began in 1962, and won the World Series a couple of times. But the Yankees and Mets had never been good at the same time. . . until 2000.

memorable performances. Many came in swimming, a competition that saw 13 new world records and a much-anticipated showdown between the United States and Australian teams. The

2000 Summer Olympics Medals

NATION	TOTAL MEDALS	NATION	TOTAL MEDALS
United States	91	France	38
Russia	89	Italy	34
China	59	Cuba	29
Australia	58	Great Britain	28
Germany	56	Netherlands	25

Other Milestones of 2000

✔ In April, American Michelle Kwan won the ladies overall title at the World Figure Skating Championships, the third of five that she would win in her career.

✔ In the Women's National Basketball Association, the Houston Comets won again . . . their fourth consecutive championship.

✔ Heavyweight Evander Holyfield became the first boxer to win the world championship four times. He beat John Ruiz August 12 to capture the World Boxing Association (WBA) title.

Evander Holyfield

✔ Controversial University of Indiana head basketball coach Bobby Knight was fired on September 10 after 29 seasons because of a "pattern of unacceptable behavior." On March 23, 2001, he was hired to coach at Texas Tech University.

✔ On December 11, All-Star shortstop Alex Rodriguez signed a 10-year, $252 million deal with the Texas Rangers. The enormous contract was the biggest ever signed in sports history. (In 2004, "A-Rod" was traded, at his request, to the New York Yankees for second baseman Alfonso Soriano.)

The first Subway Series in 44 years was cause for celebration all over New York City. The glamour of the Big Apple also excited fans around the country. An incident in Game Two added fuel to the fire. Star pitcher Roger Clemens had taken heat from the Mets for throwing too close earlier in the season. In fact, he had hit Mets star catcher Mike Piazza in a July game. So when, in Game Two, he threw one way inside to Piazza, all sorts of oddness happened. Piazza swung, and the bat broke, with the ball bouncing softly to the infield. The head of the bat, however, bounced toward Clemens, who fielded it cleanly and appeared to then throw the jagged piece of wood at Piazza as he ran down the first-base line. The incident overshadowed the game (neither player was ejected) and added to Clemens' fiery legacy.

The Series itself was decided in Game Five at Shea Stadium on October 26. In the top of the ninth with the score tied 2–2, Luis Sojo hit an RBI single off Mets starter Al Leiter, leading to a 4–2 win and the Yankees' record 26th world title.

2001

D and Controversy

The Baltimore Ravens won their first NFL championship, swamping the New York Giants 34–7 in Super Bowl XXXV on January 28. The Ravens' defense was the key, as it did not allow New York an offensive score (the Giants returned a kickoff for their only touchdown). The Ravens also created five turnovers, scored on an interception return, and held the Giants to only 152 total yards.

It was a return to NFL greatness for the city of Baltimore, though it came with a different team. The Ravens used to be the Cleveland Browns, but owner Art Modell moved that team to Baltimore in 1996. The Browns left behind the name and records of the Cleveland franchise and became the "brand-new" Ravens. Baltimore, of course, had a long history of football success, having been home to the Baltimore Colts from 1953 to 1983 before the team moved to Indianapolis (a move not approved by the NFL before it happened in the dead of night!). The multiple-city Ravens were a unique franchise in a league that proved much more stable than other pro leagues in the 2000s.

Another big story during Super Bowl XXXV week revolved around Baltimore linebacker Ray Lewis and events at the previous Super Bowl. In 2000, Lewis had attended the game as a fan. In the early morning after the game in Atlanta, he was involved in a street fight that resulted in the death of a person from a knife wound. Lewis was at first charged with attempted murder for being a part of the incident. However, over the coming months, evidence began to show that Lewis might not have been part of the crime himself. In the end, he pleaded guilty to obstruction of justice (in other words, he admitted that he had not helped police enough with their investigation). He was fined $250,000 by the NFL but was not suspended. It was a huge story at the time

Flag Day *Arizona and Colorado players hold an American flag in memory of the 9/11 attacks (page 20).*

and became a story all over again when he led the Ravens to the Super Bowl and, in fact, was named the game's MVP.

Death of Legend

The sad news continued from the world of sports at the Daytona 500 in February. On the final lap, seven-time NASCAR champion and stock-car racing legend Dale Earnhardt Sr. was clipped from behind. His car swerved to the right and hit the outer wall of the track. It did not seem at the time to be a bad wreck; hundreds of drivers have walked away from much more horrendous crashes. However, in this case, no one walked away.

Earnhardt was pronounced dead, the victim of a broken neck suffered in the crash.

The sports world was stunned. Earnhardt was the face of NASCAR for millions, a hard-driving, tough-talking man who let nothing get in his way on or off the track. He had tied Richard "The King" Petty as the all-time leader with seven NASCAR season championships. Earnhardt's black Number 3 car was far and away the most popular. His death in such a dramatic fashion—it came on the last lap as his teammate Michael Waltrip won and his son Dale Earnhardt Jr. finished second—in NASCAR's most famous race just made the event that much more noteworthy.

2001

After a long mourning period and numerous tributes from around the sports and political worlds, racing continued. In June, Dale Jr. won the Pepsi 400 at the same track on which his father had died. More importantly, the ongoing debate about safety in NASCAR racing received new energy as a result of Earnhardt's death. In the ensuing years, the sport mandated use of special head-and-neck restraints for drivers to prevent the neck-snapping movements. New walls that ab-sorbed some of the energy from crashes were also installed in many tracks. By 2007, NASCAR had redesigned the entire stock car. Beginning in 2008, all racing teams used the same basic car, which was named the Car of Tomorrow and designed from the ground up to increase driver safety.

Finally a Champion

In happier news, another veteran star athlete had a victorious ending to his career. Ray Bourque had been one of the top defensemen in the NHL for 22 years. He had played 1,825 regular-season games and been in the playoffs in 20 other seasons. But he had never held the Stan-ley Cup, the symbol of the NHL champi-onship. He had never even touched it, since hockey superstition says that a play-er can't even touch it until he wins it.

Thanks to a furious comeback by his Colorado Avalanche teammates, Bourque got his hands on the Cup this year. The Avalanche overcame a three-games-to-two deficit and beat the New Jersey Devils in seven games in the Stanley Cup Finals.

Bourque had actually left his long-time team, the Boston Bruins, two years earlier with the idea that he had only a few years left to get another shot at the Cup. The move paid off, and he won for the first time in eight tries in the Stanley Cup Finals. Fans and players alike cel-ebrated the win more for Bourque than for the Avalanche.

"In our heart, in our mind, we were playing for Ray," Avalanche coach Bob Hartley said. "This entire community was pulling for Ray. I will remember coaching Ray until the day I close my eyes."

Finally *Ray Bourque finally got a chance to hold hockey's Stanley Cup after leaving his longtime team in Boston to join the Colorado Avalanche.*

Death From Heat

Two events, one in 2001 and another two years later, led to questions about how teams and athletes should deal with heat and with dietary supplements.

On July 31, 2001, the Minnesota Vikings' 335-pound Pro Bowl lineman, Korey Stringer, collapsed during a training-camp session held in the searing heat. His body temperature was 108.8 degrees when he arrived at a hospital, where Stringer died the following day. Eighteen months later, in February 2003, Baltimore Orioles pitching prospect Steve Bechler died of heatstroke suffered during a spring training workout in Florida. The local medical examiner reported that a dietary supplement containing ephedra, which Bechler had been using, played a role in the tragedy. Ephedra was also suspected in Stringer's death, although there was no evidence that he used the substance.

As happened with Earnhardt, it took such tragedies to spur serious action by authorities. Since these events, the NFL, the NCAA, and the International Olympic Committee have banned ephedra, and Bechler's death led to calls for Major League Baseball to do the same. By 2004, President George Bush announced that the Food and Drug Administration was banning it.

Meanwhile, the families of both Bechler and Stringer went to court. Bechler's parents filed a wrongful death suit against the makers of the supplement, arguing that it was unsafe, and that the company was at fault. Stringer's widow sued the Vikings and the team doctor, holding them responsible for her husband's death. A judge dismissed her claims against the team, and she later settled with the doctor for an undisclosed sum.

One-Year Wonder

Since the NFL was born in 1920, several leagues have tried to challenge its dominance in pro football. The All-America Football Conference (AAFC) lasted only four years, 1946–49. The American Football League (AFL) did a bit better, lasting 10 years and ending up merging with the NFL in 1970. The World Football League played only in 1974–75. The United States Football League (1983–85) seemed to get off to a good start but crashed soon after in a pile of debt.

The latest challenger stepped onto the field in 2001. World Wrestling Federation founder Vince McMahon launched the XFL on February 3, 2001. The XFL boasted eight teams and a new idea: Play football in the spring, when the NFL is on vacation. The idea got a lot of atten-tion but few big-name players. Fans and television revenue did not show up as expected. The league played on, however, and on April 21, the Los Angeles Xtreme dominated the San Francisco Demons 38–6 at the Los Angeles Memorial Coliseum to win the league title in the so-called Million Dollar Game. The Xtreme became the first, and only, XFL champion. McMahon announced on May 10 that the league was folding after just one season. And the NFL remained supreme.

Barry Busts Out

When Mark McGwire and Sammy Sosa chased Roger Maris' single-season home run record in 1998, the saga electrified the sports world. Just three years later, as Barry Bonds set out on a one-man assault on McGwire's new mark

The Day the Earth Stood Still

September 11, 2001, will forever be remembered as the day when life in America underwent a dramatic and deadly change. Early that sunny morning, a horrible terrorist plot unfolded. Two commercial airplanes loaded with passengers were hijacked and deliberately slammed into the twin towers at New York City's World Trade Center. The mighty towers collapsed shortly thereafter. At about the same time, a third hijacked plane was flown into the Pentagon in Washington, D.C. A fourth plane, reportedly targeted for the U.S. Capitol building, crashed in a field in Pennsylvania after passengers overpowered the hijackers. In total, more than 3,000 people were killed as result of the terrorists' actions.

As a shocked nation mourned, everyday activities came to a virtual standstill. Cancellations in the sports world included baseball games for six days, a week of NFL and college football games, NASCAR, golf, and other major events. "At a certain point," said NFL commissioner Paul Tagliabue, "playing our games can contribute to the healing process. Just not at this time." When the action did resume, special homage was paid to the victims at venues nationwide, and strict new security measures were instituted.

Responsibility for the attacks was claimed by members of the Al Qaeda terrorist network, based largely in Afghanistan and led by Osama bin Laden. On October 7, sports broadcasts were interrupted as President George W. Bush announced the beginning of Operation Enduring Freedom, an American-led military action in Afghanistan to overthrow the Taliban government, which supported Al Qaeda's efforts, and to destroy terrorist operations in the country.

The effects of 9/11 continue even to today. "God Bless America" is sung during the seventh-inning stretch at many Major League Baseball games. Servicemen and women are often honored at pro games. Perhaps the most famous sports-related 9/11 story was that of Pat Tillman, an NFL star who was inspired by the events of the day to leave his career behind and join the military (see page 46).

of 70 dingers, the level of attention was quite a bit less. Bonds, though amazingly talented and already a three-time Most Valuable Player (on his way to a record seven MVPs), had a prickly personality and was hard to love.

Still, his home-run power was impossible to ignore. Even as manager after manager intentionally walked him, he still managed to find enough times at bat to hit homers. Bonds had 156 hits that year . . . nearly half were home runs.

Bonds actually started the season slowly, but then hit several hot streaks. He hit an N.L.-record nine homers in five games in May. His 37 homers by the All-Star break were tied for the most ever to that point. By early September, he had cruised past 60. His march was delayed as baseball shut down for a week after 9/11 (see sidebar), but when the sport re-started, he quickly became the focus.

Bonds faced another challenge when the games began again. He did chip away and add homers, but not in bunches. Along with an almost-hostile press and indifferent fans, he battled managers who pitched around him. In one series against the Houston Astros, he was walked intentionally eight times in 14 trips to the plate. In the 15th at-bat of that series, however, he hit his 70th of the season, tying McGwire. In his next game, now back home in San Francisco in front of the only people in America who truly loved him, he set the new mark with number 71 against the archrival Los Angeles Dodgers. He added two more to place the bar, probably out of reach now in the post-steroid era, at 73.

While Bonds earned a spot in the record books, by the end of the decade, he was looking less like a hero and more like the opposite. Looking back at his record season from 2009, it's hard to remember that even back then the issue of steroid use or performance-enhancing drugs was more of a myth or a rumor than full-blown controversy. So as Bonds smashed homer after homer in 2001, people were amazed and thrilled . . . but not really suspicious. That would come later. In 2001, the baseball world simply cheered, though perhaps not as loudly as it could have.

Drama at the World Series

The events of 9/11 were still sadly fresh in America's mind when the World Series began on October 27. The temporary shutdown in baseball had pushed the starting date later than ever before. Along with patriotic songs before and during the games, before Game Three, President George W. Bush famously took the mound to throw out the first pitch at Yankee Stadium, in the same city where the terrorists had struck about two

On Record Pace *San Francisco Giants slugger Barry Bonds connects off a San Diego Padres pitcher for one of what would become an all-time record 73 home runs in the 2001 season.*

2001

months earlier. His appearance was another sign that America was bouncing back from the tragedy, that traditions would continue, and that he and we would show a brave face to terror.

As for the games, the Yankees were facing the upstart Arizona Diamondbacks, the National League champions in only their fourth season of existence. The action on the field proved to be among the most dramatic and memorable in World Series history, adding athletic luster to an emotional event.

Arizona won the first two games at home, led by their one-two starting-pitcher punch of Randy Johnson and Curt Schilling. After Bush's dramatic appearance, the Yankees won Game Three behind Roger "Rocket" Clemens. In Game Four, drama appeared again when Tino Martinez hit a two-run homer in the bottom of the ninth and Derek Jeter hit a solo shot in the 10th to give the Yankees a walk-off win. Game Five provided another hero, Scott Brosius, whose two-run, ninth-inning homer tied the game. The Yankees went on to win in 12 innings.

Game Six was back in Arizona and, perhaps spent from the drama in the Bronx, the Yankees were thumped

Other Milestones of 2001

✔ At the Masters in Augusta, Georgia in April, Tiger Woods held on to win the first major of the year for the second time. Including his victories in the 2000 U.S. and British Opens and PGA Championship, he became the first golfer to hold all four major tournament titles at the same time.

✔ Running great Jim Ryun's 36-year-old high school record in the mile (3:55.3, June 27, 1965) was snapped on May 27 by 18-year-old Alan Webb, who ran the distance in 3:53.43 at the Prefontaine Classic in Oregon.

Major League Lacrosse

✔ Ali and Frazier met again on June 8 at Turning Stone Casino in Verona, New York, when the daughters of the boxing rivals (Muhammad Ali and Joe Frazier fought three of the most famous bouts in his-

tory in the 1970s) squared off. Laila Ali outlasted Jacqui Frazier-Lyde over eight rounds for the victory.

✔ In July, American cycling star Lance Armstrong won his third straight Tour de France.

✔ Venus Williams successfully defended her Wimbledon and U.S. Open titles in 2001. At the Open, she and runnerup Serena Williams became the first sisters to meet in a Grand Slam final since Wimbledon in 1884.

✔ Major League Lacrosse began play as the first pro U.S. outdoor lacrosse league. MLL, in which all teams are owned by the league itself, had grown to six teams by 2009, mostly in East Coast cities.

15–2, as Arizona tied the Series at three victories apiece.

Game Seven gathered up all the emotion of the week and the games and ratcheted it up a notch further. Yankees ace Roger Clemens and Schilling locked into a pitcher's duel that left the score 2–1 late in the game. Johnson, the fireballing superstar, came into the game in relief of Schilling. Johnson had pitched and won Game Six the night before, but his team needed some outs. He held the Yankees in check to give the Diamondbacks a chance.

They got their chance and came through in the ninth against New York's ace closer, Mariano Rivera. A lead-off single, a fielder's choice, and an error put a runner on third in a game the Yankees led 2–1. Tony Womack then doubled home the tying run as the Arizona fans went nuts. A few batters later, the bases were loaded with one out. The Yankees' infield came in to cut down a possible winning run. But Luis Gonzalez blooped a single over shortstop Jeter's head, and the Diamondbacks scored, earning their first World Series title in dramatic fashion.

The Series was historic. Johnson set a postseason record with five victories. He and Schilling were named the Series co-MVPs, the first time a pair of pitchers had earned that honor. It was the first time that so many games had ended on walk-off hits. It was the third time that the home team won every game in the Series. In Game Seven, Arizona became the first

Series Winner *Luis Gonzalez of the Arizona Diamondbacks sliced the final, game-winning hit of a dramatic and historic World Series in the bottom of the ninth inning of Game 7.*

team to trail going into the bottom of the ninth and win the game and the championship. And, of course, this thrilling, positive, exciting event brightened the shadows of tragedy that had darkened the world.

2002

Patriots Days

Less than four months after the tragedy of 9/11, Americans were inspired by a patriotic display of entertainment at Super Bowl XXXVI in the Louisiana Superdome in New Orleans on February. And while no football game ever could make up for the horrifying events of that day in September, the nation's spirits were lifted a bit by a classic Super Bowl that was the first ever to be decided as time ran out. The last play was a 48-yard field goal by Adam Vinatieri that gave upstart New England a 20–17 victory over the heavily favored St. Louis Rams.

The Patriots' surprise ride to their first NFL championship began when Tom Brady, an unheralded sixth-round draft pick from Michigan in 2000, stepped in for injured Drew Bledsoe early in the season. With Brady at the controls, New England overcame an 0–2 start to win 11 of its last 14 games and take the AFC East.

Still, the Patriots' season appeared over when, trailing the Oakland Raiders 13–10 late in the fourth quarter of a divisional playoff game in New England, Brady apparently lost a fumble to end his team's last chance. But in what has come to be know as the "Tuck Rule," the loose ball was ruled an incomplete pass after a replay review because a quarterback that drops a ball, even if in the process of tucking the ball back in to his body, is simulating a throwing motion. The Patriots retained possession, and Vinatieri eventually booted a 45-yard field goal through a driving snowstorm to force overtime. In the extra session, his 23-yard kick won it.

After the Patriots beat the Pittsburgh Steelers in the AFC Championship Game, they faced the Rams in the Super Bowl. St. Louis, which won Super Bowl XXXIV two seasons earlier, featured a high-powered offense that was the first in NFL history to score more than 500 points in three consecutive seasons.

But with the Patriots utilizing a ball-control offense and a bend-but-don't-break defense, the game was tied at 17–17 late in the fourth quarter. Brady, operating without time outs, then needed only 83 seconds to march his team from its own 17-yard line to the Rams' 30. Vinatieri came on with seven seconds remaining to make his winning kick, and set off a celebration of confetti inside the Superdome. Fittingly, the confetti was colored red, white, and blue.

Super Bowl First *Adam Vinatieri's field goal was the first to win a Super Bowl on the final play of the game.*

Salt Lake City Games

Scandals notwithstanding (see box on page 27), the enduring memory of the Winter Olympic Games that began in Salt Lake City February 8 was the gold medal won by 16-year-old American Sarah Hughes in women's figure skating.

Michelle Kwan (b.1980), the holder of four world and six U.S. titles, and the silver medalist at the 1998 Games in Na-gano, Japan, was expected to finally mine Olympic gold in Salt Lake City. But Kwan fell during the long program and finished with a bronze medal. And just as teenager Tara Lipinski skated away with the gold medal in Nagano, Hughes leapfrogged from fourth place after the short program to win.

Jim Shea claimed a bittersweet victory in the men's skeleton event, which hadn't been in the Olympics since 1948.

2002

After sliding face down on a sleek fiberglass sled along the curvy bobsled track at 80 miles per hour, a triumphant Shea held up a picture of his grandfather to the television cameras. Jack Shea, who won two gold medals in speed skating at the 1932 Olympics in Lake Placid, New York, had died just a few weeks earlier at the age of 91. But his son, Jim Sr.—a cross-country skiing competitor at the 1964 Games in Innsbruck, Austria—was in Salt Lake to congratulate the youngest member of America's first three-generation family of Winter Olympians.

A Golden Smile *American skater Sarah Hughes overcame several more-famous rivals to capture the gold medal at the 2002 Winter Olympics.*

In all, the United States won 10 gold medals at the XIX Winter Games, including an historic victory for Vonetta Flowers in the first women's Olympic bobsled event. When she and teammate Jill Bakken claimed victory, Vonetta became the first black person ever to win an Olympic Winter Games gold medal.

Lakers Three-peat

The Los Angeles Lakers won the NBA championship for the third season in a row, easily beating the Eastern Conference-champion New Jersey Nets in four games. The deciding contest officially was a 113–107 victory in New Jersey on June 12 in a game in which Finals MVP Shaquille O'Neal scored 34 points and grabbed 10 rebounds, and Kobe Bryant added 25 points and 8 assists.

For all intents and purposes, though, the Lakers can point to a game three weeks earlier, on May 26, that really helped earn them their third consecutive title. That night, on the verge of facing an almost-insurmountable three-games-to-one deficit to the Pacific Division-champion Sacramento Kings, forward Robert Horry sank a dramatic buzzer-beating three-point shot for a 100–99 victory at the Staples Center in Los Angeles to even the series at two games apiece. It was the fourth playoff series in a row over a span of two seasons that Horry made a game-winning three-pointer.

To the Kings' credit, they rebounded to win Game Five in Sacramento, but the Lakers took a pair of close decisions in the final two games to win the series and advance to the Finals.

Olympic Scandals

Scandal rocked the Olympic movement in November 1998 when it was alleged that International Olympic Committee members had been bribed by Salt Lake City, Utah, officials to influence the city's selection as the site for the 2002 Winter Games. An investigation prompted the resignations of two top Salt Lake Olympic Organizing Committee executives and several IOC members, as well as sweeping reforms throughout the IOC, based in Lausanne, Switzerland. (In early 2004, a Utah judge threw out the case against the U.S. official who was charged, citing lack of evidence. However, the IOC reforms remained in place.)

The IOC storm had subsided by the time the 2002 Winter Games began in Salt Lake City, but then a different type of problem arose, in the pairs figure skating event. Soon after Russians Elena Berezhnaya and Anton Sikharulidze narrowly won the gold medal over a seemingly superior duo from Canada, David Pelletier and Jamie Sale, a scandal erupted. It was determined that the French judge's vote had been biased—she had allegedly agreed to vote the Russians up in exchange for another judge's vote for a French pair. An unprecedented second set of golds was awarded to the Canadians six days later.

Americans Get Their Kicks

The new and the old came together at soccer's World Cup, held in South Korea and Japan from May 31 to June 30. The new: For the first time, the International Federation of Association Football's (FIFA) premier event was held in Asia. And for the first time, host duties were shared by two countries. The old: For the fifth time in the 17 World Cups to date, it was Brazil, led by brilliant play of striker Ronaldo, that took home the Jules Rimet Trophy as the team champion. Ronaldo scored both goals in Brazil's 2–0 victory over Germany in the final in Yokohama, Japan.

While Brazil clearly was the class of the World Cup, American soccer fans were buoyed by an excellent performance from the U.S. team. After the United States dropped all three of its matches in the 1998 World Cup, little was expected from head coach Bruce Arena's team in Asia. But in their first match, the Americans pulled off a stunning 3–2 upset of Portugal, one of the pre-tournament favorites. That helped propel the United States into the knockout stage, where a 2–0 victory over Mexico earned the Americans a berth in the quarterfinals.

Although their dreams of a World Cup victory were dashed by Germany 1–0 in that round, the Americans had scored another major victory for the visibility of soccer in the United States.

Fit to Be Tied

When the decision was made, Major League Baseball Commissioner Bud Selig could only throw up his hands as if to say, "What else can we do?" Baseball fans could only throw up their hands in disgust. Selig had just declared the All-Star Game at Miller Park in Milwaukee on July 9 a tie.

In 2002, baseball already had fought the bad memories of the long, bitter strike by players in 1994, which cancelled that

2002

year's playoffs and World Series. Those memories resurfaced as another work stoppage threatened to wreck the 2002 season. Luckily, the players and owners agreed on a new collective bargaining agreement just hours before the August 31 deadline.

But then came the All-Star Game. In an exciting, back-and-forth game, the American League scored four runs in the top of the seventh inning to take a 6–5 lead, only to see the National League counter with two runs in the bottom of the seventh for a 7–6 advantage. After the American League scored again in the eighth to make it 7–7, neither side could push across a tie-breaking run.

After 11 innings, both sides ran out of pitchers, and the umpires consulted Selig. After his decision, fans were outraged. MLB reacted by declaring that the outcome of future games would have real meaning: The winner of the annual Mid-summer Classic would determine home-

A Beaming Beem *Rich Beem became the first player to hold off a charging Tiger Woods in a major tournament when he won the 2002 PGA Championship and this gleaming trophy.*

field advantage for the World Series (the advantage previously alternated between leagues each year).

Do a Little Dance

After the final putt dropped, Rich Beem did a little dance, right there on the 18th green. A virtual unknown when the 84th PGA Championship began on August 15 at the Hazeltine National Golf Club in Chaska, Minnesota, the former car-stereo and cell-phone salesman stunned the golf world by holding off Tiger Woods to win the first (and to date, only) major championship of his career.

Beem entered the final round three strokes behind leader Justin Leonard, with Woods lurking two shots behind him. But Beem quickly erased his deficit to Leonard, then took control of the tournament with a brilliant eagle on the 11th hole. On the 16th hole, he drained a 35-foot putt for birdie to hold off the hard-charging Woods, who birdied the last four holes, by one shot.

Then came the hula-like, celebration dance on the final hole. "I probably looked like a total idiot out there," Beem admitted, "but you know what? I won."

Sister, Sister

Venus Williams was the top-ranked women's tennis player in the world in 2001, but all the while she insisted that younger sister Serena was closing in. Sure enough, it was Serena who ascended to the top in 2002.

That year, the sisters met in three consecutive Grand Slam finals—the

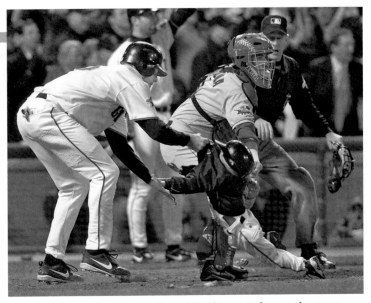

Save for a First Baseman *One of the biggest plays at the 2002 World Series involved J.T. Snow (left) and batboy Darren Baker (being grabbed), son of the Giants manager.*

French Open, Wimbledon, and the U.S. Open—with Serena winning all three. The 21-year-old Serena ended the season as the top-ranked player in the world, with the 22-year-old Venus second.

Tennis fans would see a lot more of the amazing Williams sisters throughout the decade.

J.T. Snow's Biggest Play

One of the lingering images of the 2002 World Series came in Game Five at AT&T Park in San Francisco. In the seventh inning of the Giants' 16–4 rout, Kenny Lofton hit a one-out triple with two men aboard. First baseman J.T. Snow scored, with third baseman David Bell in close pursuit.

But when Snow crossed the plate, he noticed the flash of a little Giant near home plate in front of Bell. It was

Running into History *Already a legend for helping the Cowboys win three Super Bowls, Emmitt Smith secured his place in history be becoming the NFL's all-time leading rusher.*

NFL's All-Time Rushing Leaders

Here's the progression of the NFL's all-time rushing mark. Note: The NFL began in 1920, but individual statistics were not kept until 1932.

PLAYER	*YEAR	YARDS
Cliff Battles	1932	3,511
Clarke Hinkle	1940	3,860
Steve Van Buren	1949	5,860
Joe Perry	1958	8,378
Jim Brown	1963	12,312
Walter Payton	1984	16,726
Emmitt Smith	2002	18,355

*The year the player became the NFL's all-time leading rusher.

three-year-old Darren Baker, the son of manager Dusty Baker and the team's batboy that night. Darren was a little too eager to pick up Lofton's bat and was in harm's way with the ball, Bell, and Angels catcher Bengie Molina all converging near the plate.

In one motion, Snow reached back, grabbed Darren by the collar of his Giants' jacket, and lifted him to safety. It may have been the biggest play of Snow's long career.

Heavenly Comeback

The Anaheim Angels were World Series champions for the first time after staging one of the most remarkable comebacks in the history of the Fall Classic to beat the National League-champion San Francisco Giants in seven games.

The Angels were down three games to two and trailed Game Six in Anaheim 5–0 in the bottom of the seventh inning on October 26. No team ever had rallied from five runs down in an elimination game, let alone with only eight outs of life left. But Scott Spiezio's one-out, three-run home run brought the Angels close. Then, Troy Glaus' two-run double was the key hit in a three-run eighth inning that gave Anaheim a 6–5 win.

The next night, rookie John Lackey shut down the Barry Bonds-led Giants on four hits over five innings of a 4–1 victory.

New Rushing King

The Dallas Cowboys, the NFL's dominant team of the 1990s, slogged through their third consecutive five-win

Other Milestones of 2002

✔ Maryland won the NCAA Men's Basketball Tournament for the first time, beating Indiana 64–52 in the final game on April 1 in Atlanta. One night earlier, in San Antonio, Connecticut capped an undefeated season by beating Oklahoma 82–70 for the women's title.

✔ The Detroit Red Wings won the Stanley Cup for the third time in six years, beating the surprising Carolina Hurricanes, who were making their first appearance in the Finals, four games to one. The final game was a 3–1 victory in Detroit June 13. The win marked the record ninth career Stanley Cup win for Red Wings coach Scotty Bowman, who announced his retirement.

✔ On July 30, in a game against the Miami Sol, Los Angeles Sparks star Lisa Leslie became the first player ever to dunk in a WNBA game.

✔ The United States Men's National Basketball Team finished a disappointing sixth at the International Basketball Federation (FIBA) World Championships in Indianapolis in the summer. Yugoslavia, featuring Dallas Mavericks star Dirk Nowitzki, downed the NBA-laden American team in the Knockout Stage and went on to win the title.

Lisa Leslie

✔ Tennis' Pete Sampras won the 14th, and final, major championship of his career when he beat rival Andre Agassi in four sets in the U.S. Open final September 8. At 31, Sampras was the oldest winner of the Open in more than 30 years.

✔ On September 14, American Tim Montgomery set a world record by running the 100 meters in 9.78 seconds in Paris. Three years later, though, the record was vacated after Montgomery was found to be using performance-enhancing drugs.

✔ Boston Red Sox Hall of Famer Ted Williams, one of the greatest hitters in baseball history, died of cardiac arrest July 5. His body was preserved by a method of freezing called cryonics. Other notable deaths in 2002: golfing great Sam Snead (age 89) and football star Johnny Unitas (age 69).

---

season of the 2000s, but did have one major bright spot during a 17–14 loss to the Seattle Seahawks on October 27. That day, 33-year-old Emmitt Smith surpassed Walter Payton as the NFL's all-time leading rusher.

The legendary Payton rushed for 16,726 yards in 13 seasons with the Chicago Bears from 1975 to 1987. Smith, in his 13th season in 2002, entered the game against Seattle 92 yards short of the all-

time mark. A little more than five minutes into the fourth quarter, he took a handoff and burst 11 yards up the middle to set the record.

Smith, a first-round draft choice out of Florida who helped lead the Cowboys to three Super Bowl championships in the nineties, played the 2003 and 2004 seasons with the Arizona Cardinals. He finished his 15-year career with 18,355 rushing yards.

2003

Undisputed Champ...Sort Of

For once, there was no arguing that the two best teams in college football were playing for the national championship when the 12–0 and top-ranked Miami Hurricanes played the 13–0 and number-two-rated Ohio State Buckeyes in the Fiesta Bowl in Tempe, Arizona, for the BCS title on January 4. Still, what would college football in the 2000s be without controversy? Ohio State's 31–24 victory in two overtimes was tinged with debate after a crucial pass-interference call in the end zone helped determine the outcome.

The defending-champion Hurricanes took a 24–17 lead in the first overtime on quarterback Ken Dorsey's seven-yard touchdown pass to tight end Kellen Winslow Jr. (In college football, unlike in the NFL, overtime is not sudden death, or "sudden victory." Instead, teams each have one possession beginning at the opponents' 25-yard line to try to break the tie; if the game is still tied after that, they do it again.)

The Buckeyes soon faced a fourth down at the five-yard line on their possession. Quarterback Craig Krenzel threw a pass for receiver Chris Gamble in the end zone. The ball, Gamble, and Miami

defensive back Glenn Sharpe all arrived at just about the same time. The ball fell to the ground, and Hurricanes' players began celebrating their victory as fireworks went off above Sun Devil Stadium.

Then, everyone noticed the penalty flag. Sharpe was called for pass interference, and the Buckeyes had a fresh set of downs. They soon tied the game on Krenzel's one-yard run, took the lead on the first possession in the next overtime when Maurice Clarett ran five yards for a touchdown, and won it by stopping Miami on its last chance.

For the Hurricanes, the end to their 34-game winning streak was extra difficult because they thought they already had won. The key penalty flag had been thrown late because, as field judge Terry Porter later explained, "I replayed it in my mind. I wanted to make double sure it was the right call."

To this day, Ohio State fans believe it was the right call. Miami Hurricanes fans do not.

Another Barrier Broken

 Businessman Robert L. Johnson became the first African-American

Hero on Wheels *Lance Armstrong won his fifth Tour de France, equaling an all-time record (page 37).*

majority owner of a major professional sports franchise in the United States when the NBA approved his purchase of the expansion Charlotte Bobcats franchise on January 10. Johnson also became the owner of the WNBA's Charlotte Sting.

Johnson made his fortune as the founder of the cable channel Black Entertainment Television (BET), which debuted in 1980. He sold BET to Viacom for $3 billion in 2001 and became the nation's first African-American billionaire. That year, he also became the first African-American to be named on a Forbes magazine "World's Richest" list.

The Bobcats, whose ownership group now also includes legendary basketball star Michael Jordan, began play in the Southeast Division of the NBA's Eastern Conference in the 2004–05 NBA season.

Sound Investment

Tampa Bay Buccaneers owner Malcolm Glazer was so intent on getting Jon Gruden to coach his NFL team that he took the unusual step of obtaining him from the Oakland Raiders (the team Gruden coached from 1998 to 2001) via a trade in 2002. And not only that, but the price was steep: four draft picks, including two first-round selections, and $8 million in cash. But Glazer's investment quickly paid off when Gruden led the Buccaneers to their first Super Bowl victory in game XXXVII on January 26, 2003, in San Diego.

For several years, the Buccaneers had been good but not great. They made the playoffs four times in five seasons beginning in 1997, and never finished below .500 in that span. But they could not make the next step to the Super Bowl, and Glazer did not want the window of opportunity to close on a team that featured stars such as fullback Mike Alstott and linebacker Derrick Brooks. Under Gruden's guidance, Tampa Bay cruised to a division title with 12 victories during the regular season in 2002, then was not challenged much in the playoffs early in the 2003 calendar year.

Even the Buccaneers' victory in the Super Bowl was a rout. Coincidentally, Tampa Bay's 48–21 win came over Gruden's former team, the Raiders.

One Loss Doesn't Hurt

A stunning thing happened to the University of Connecticut women's basketball team in 2003: The Huskies lost a game. Still, that didn't stop them from winning their second consecutive national championship with a 73–68 victory over rival Tennessee in Atlanta on April 8.

Head coach Geno Auriemma's Connecticut team didn't have a senior on the roster, but still cruised through a perfect regular season in which it built its winning streak to a record 70 games entering the Big East Conference Tournament championship game against Villanova. The 14th-ranked Wildcats, however, slowed down the game and stunned Connecticut 52–48, ending the Huskies' long winning streak and a string of nine consecutive Big East Tournament titles.

"Maybe this is the best thing that could happen to us," Auriemma said, as

Taking It to the 'Net

Sports media and fandom began to change in the 1990s with the advent of the personal computer and the Internet. By 2003, virtually every major and minor sport, league, team, and player was represented on multiple Web sites loaded with news, statistics, photos, video clips, history, and everything else ravenous visitors could digest. Fans also gobbled up Web versions of brand names such as ESPN.com and SportsIllustrated.com, as well as online editions of niche sports media. You name it—lacrosse, Olympics, water polo, horse racing, snowboarding, kite surfing, soccer, bass fishing, ad infinitum— you could find it somewhere on the Internet.

The majority of U.S. homes had access to the Internet by then, putting the medium on the verge of replacing newspapers, magazines, and even television as the primary source of sports news and entertainment. High-speed access, via DSL lines or cable modems, promised infinite options for online fans.

Huskies on Top *Coach Gino Auriemma holds up the NCAA trophy just won by his University of Connecticut women's basketball team, capping off one of the best seasons ever.*

the pressure of the win streak was behind his team. That turned out to be a wise prediction. The Huskies still were a top seed in the NCAA Tournament, and they had little trouble reaching the Final Four. There, they overcame Texas and Tennessee in close games to win the title.

Masters Protest

Canadian Mike Weir's one-hole playoff victory over Len Mattiace in the Masters golf tournament April 13 was overshadowed by an attention-getting protest over women's rights outside the

exclusive Augusta, Georgia, golf course during the week.

The opening move in the protest was fired in June 2002 when Martha Burk, head of the National Council of Women's Organizations, sent a letter to Augusta National Golf Club chairman William "Hootie" Johnson. Burk's group urged that the men-only club admit women members for the first time in its 70-year history. Johnson steadfastly refused, and a heated national debate ensued. The basic issue: women's rights to equal access versus a private club's right to control its membership.

2003

The controversy came to a head—sort of—on day three of the tournament. Burk led a smaller-than-expected group of protesters outside the club, while a handful of Augusta supporters, curious onlookers, and a CBS television audience (watching the tournament commercial-free after Johnson voided sponsorships) looked on.

Historic Sorenstam *Already a superstar on the women's golf tour, Annika Sorenstam made history by taking part in a men's tournament (and later a Skins Game against men). Though she missed the cut in the tournament, she struck a blow for equality in sports.*

In the end, Augusta National remained all-male (and does to this day). Meanwhile, the most effective endorsement for women's equality in golf came, fittingly, on the golf course. In May, Annika Sorenstam became the first woman golfer to play in a men's PGA Tour event since 1945—she missed the cut at the Bank of America Colonial but won the adulation of the galleries. In November, she became the first woman ever to play in the Skins Game, where she finished in second place while earning $225,000 in the annual postseason event.

The Police Blotter Spreads

In 2003, two major off-the-basketball-court incidents underscored the troubling trend of athletes making headlines for all the wrong reasons. On July 4, Los Angeles Lakers superstar Kobe Bryant was arrested on suspicion of sexual assault. And late in July, former Baylor University basketball player Carlton Dotson was arrested and charged with the murder of a teammate.

In the latter incident, Baylor basketball player Patrick Dennehy was reported missing on June 19, 2003, and foul play was immediately suspected. In late July, two days after friend and teammate Dotson was arrested and charged with Dennehy's murder, the body was found in Waco, Texas.

On July 4, 2003, officials in Eagle County, Colorado, arrested Bryant, 24, on suspicion of sexually assaulting a 19-year-old woman who worked at a resort where Bryant was staying. On July 18, he was formally charged, and in an emotional press conference later that day admitted to having sex with his accuser, with her consent, he believed. (In September of 2004, the charges against Bryant were dropped after his accuser told prosecutors that she was unwilling to testify. Bryant and his accuser also settled a civil lawsuit over the incident.)

Bryant's very public image—as a clean-cut member of three NBA-championship teams with the Lakers and as a highly paid pitchman for McDonald's, Coca-Cola, and Nike—fueled a major media circus, as well as the ongoing debate over the role and treatment of athletes in society.

Facing the Music *Lakers star Kobe Bryant, with his wife Vanessa at this side, faced tough questions about his actions at a Colorado hotel, actions which nearly sent him to court.*

Tour de Lance

As Lance Armstrong took his ceremonial ride along the Champs-Elysees in Paris on July 27, 2003, and crossed the finish line after the 20th and final stage of the world's toughest and most celebrated bicycle race, he joined a very exclusive club. Wearing the leader's yellow jersey, the 31-year-old Texan, racing for the U.S. Postal Service team, had just won his fifth Tour de France. Only four others in the 90 Tours run to that point had won as many (the event was first held in 1903, but was interrupted during both World Wars). Adding to the grandeur of the moment, Armstrong became just the second rider to claim five Tours in a row, joining Spain's Miguel Indurain (b.1964), who dominated from 1991 to 1995. "It's a dream, really a dream," Armstrong said in French from the winner's podium.

All five of Armstrong's victories have been remarkable—they came after a near-fatal fight with cancer in 1996—but this one took on mythical proportions. He suffered through the stomach flu just before the three-week, 2,130-mile race began on July 5; he survived bumps and bruises from two crashes; he narrowly avoided a potentially disastrous spill in the mountains. Plus, the competition had never been so tight.

Armstrong finished a scant 61 seconds ahead of five-time runner-up Jan Ullrich of Germany, whose hopes had tumbled along with his bike on a rain-soaked road during a crucial time trial the day before. The close finish was historic; Armstrong's previous margins of victory had all been more than six minutes. "I think this year I had to rely more on strategy than on physical gifts or physical fitness," he stated.

Armstrong pledged to be back in 2004. "I love cycling, I love my job, and I will be back for a sixth," he said.

The Chicago Curse *When Cubs fan Steve Bartman (in blue hat) reached out for a souvenir in this playoff game, he never imagined what would happen as a result. Moises Alou came down without the ball, and the Cubs left the series without another win.*

Curses, Foiled Again!

With even casual baseball fans eagerly anticipating the matchup, and network TV executives excited about the idea, the American League Boston Red Sox and the National League Chicago Cubs appeared destined to break decades of frustration and disappointment and meet in the World Series in 2003.

Alas, each club's historic curse reared its ugly head at just about the last, and worst, possible moment—in each league's respective championship series—and the dream World Series never came to pass. Instead, the upstart Florida Marlins flouted tradition by whipping the 26-time-champion New York Yankees in six games in the World Series in October. The finale was a five-hit, 2–0 gem by 23-year-old Florida right-hander Josh Beckett.

Boston ended 2003 still trying to shake the Curse of the Bambino: Not long after winning the World Series in 1918, the club sold Babe Ruth to the Yankees and hadn't won a Fall Classic since.

The Red Sox were on the verge of returning to baseball's premier stage for the first time since 1986 when they took a 5–2 lead into the bottom of the eighth inning behind pitching ace Pedro Martinez in game seven of the A.L. Championship Series (ALCS) at Yankee Stadium. But the Yankees rallied to tie the game, then went on to win in the 11th inning on Aaron Boone's solo home run.

Over in the National League, the Cubs still haven't won a World Series championship since 1908 or even a league pennant since the 1945 season—the Cubs' alleged curse involves a goat denied ad-

Other Milestones of 2003

✔ Ricky Craven beat Kurt Busch at the Carolina Dodge Dealers 400 on March 16 in the closest finish in NASCAR history. Craven won by .002 seconds; he hit the finish line a matter of inches ahead of his rival.

✔ Syracuse, led by freshman sensation (and future NBA star) Carmelo Anthony, beat Kansas 81–78 in the title game in New Orleans on April 7 to win the NCAA Men's Basketball Championship.

✔ Yankees right-hander Roger Clemens reached two of pitching's elite career milestones—300 victories and 4,000 strikeouts—during a 5–2 win over the St. Louis Cardinals in New York on June 13. Clemens became the 21st pitcher to win 300 and only the third to fan 4,000.

✔ After beating the Los Angeles Lakers in the Western Conference semifinals and the Dallas Mavericks in the conference finals, the San Antonio Spurs eliminated the New Jersey Nets in six games in the NBA Finals in June. An 88–77 home-court victory on June 15 at the SBC Center marked the Spurs' second NBA title.

✔ In the first Major League Baseball All-Star Game with home-field advantage in the World Series at

NASCAR's closest finish ever

stake, the American League beat the National League 7–6 on July 15 at the home of the Chicago White Sox. Texas Rangers third baseman Hank Blalock hit a two-out, two-run home run in the bottom of the eighth inning off Los Angeles Dodgers closer Eric Gagne to make the difference.

✔ Heralded 18-year-old phenom LeBron James made his NBA debut for the Cleveland Cavaliers at Sacramento on October 29. James scored 25 points, grabbed 6 rebounds, and handed out 9 assists, but the Kings won 106–92.

---

mission to the 1945 Series—but new manager Dusty Baker and a talented young pitching staff carried the Cubs to the N.L. Central title in the 2003 season. After beating the Braves in the Division Series, Chicago jumped on Florida, winning three of the first four games and, after dropping Game Five, taking a 3-0 lead into the eighth inning of the potential pennant-clincher at Wrigley Field. That's when Chicago fan Steve Bartman, cheering his beloved team from a front-row seat down the left-field line, instinctively reached for a foul fly ball—and inadvertently kept

Cubs left fielder Moises Alou from catching it. There was no official interference (the ball was in the stands) and it should have been a footnote. Instead, batter Luis Castillo, given new life, walked. After four hits, a couple of walks, a critical error, and a sacrifice fly, an astonishing eight runs had crossed the plate. Thousands of fans jammed onto Wavefield and Sheffield Avenues, not to mention the 39,577 inside Wrigley Field, went home stunned. The Marlins won 9–6 the next night to advance to the World Series.

2004

Another BCS Mess

The Bowl Championship Series (BCS) was supposed to settle the argument over who was No. 1 in college football, but it has regularly only added to the debate. That was never more evident than in 2004, when two schools—the Louisiana State Tigers and the Southern California Trojans (USC)—each claimed national championships for the year.

In the weeks leading up to the BCS title game, it appeared as if the top-ranked and undefeated Oklahoma Sooners and No. 2 USC were heading for a showdown. But when Oklahoma was routed by Kansas State 35–7 in the Big 12 Championship Game, the Trojans ascended to the top spot in the polls and prepared to meet the second-ranked Tigers for the national crown.

The complicated BCS formula, however, spit out Oklahoma, now ranked third in the polls, and Louisiana State as the two teams to play for the title, while No. 1 USC went to the Rose Bowl to play the No. 4 Michigan Wolverines.

In Pasadena on January 1, the Trojans easily handled the Wolverines 28–14. Three nights later, at the Sugar Bowl in New Orleans, Louisiana State shut down Oklahoma's high-powered offense in a 21–14 victory.

The Tigers thus were the BCS champions. But the Associated Press kept USC at No. 1 in its final poll and declared the Trojans the national champions.

Twice As Nice for UConn

The University of Connecticut pulled off a rare basketball double by winning both the men's and women's NCAA Basketball Tournaments.

Jim Calhoun's men's team was far from perfect most of the season, but the Huskies were at their best when it counted the most. UConn lost six games during the regular portion of the schedule, but then swept through the rugged Big East Conference Tournament to earn a No. 2 seed at the NCAAs. After breezing through the West region with four victories of at least 16 points each, the Huskies were on the verge of falling to Atlantic Coast Conference power Duke in the national semifinal game on April 3 in San Antonio.

But center Emeka Okafor, who soon would be the No. 2 overall pick in the 2004 NBA draft (by the Charlotte Bobcats),

Victory Dance *The Boston Red Sox joyously celebrated a World Series title . . . and the end of a curse (page 45).*

asserted himself down the stretch. He scored all 18 of his points in the second half, and the Huskies erased an eight-point deficit in the final minutes to win 79–78. Two nights later, Okafor was a monster, pouring in 24 points and grabbing 15 rebounds in an 82–73 win over Georgia Tech in the title game.

In New Orleans on April 6, head coach Geno Auriemma's UConn women's

2004 team won its third consecutive national title with a 70–61 victory over Tennessee in the championship game. It was the second year in a row that the Huskies beat their biggest rival in the final game. Guard Diana Taurasi earned the Most Outstanding Player award in the Final Four for the second year in a row.

Phinally . . . Phil *Golfer Phil Mickelson exults after his final putt clinched a victory in the Masters, his first victory in a major tournament. He was the first lefthanded player to win the event.*

Stamp of Approval

For a long time, Phil Mickelson was called the "best golfer never to win a Major." He finally shed that undesirable tag with a one-stroke victory at the Masters Tournament at the Augusta (Georgia) National Golf Club on April 11.

The 34-year-old Mickelson, the PGA Tour's most consistent winner this side of Tiger Woods, had teed it up 46 times in golf's most important tournaments—the Masters, the U.S. Open, the British Open, and the PGA Championship—but came up short each time. It looked like it might be another good-but-not-good-enough performance in 2004 when he entered the final round on Sunday tied for the lead, only to shoot two-over-par on the front nine. Beginning on the 12th hole, though, he caught fire. He birdied four of the next six holes and headed to 18 tied for the lead with Ernie Els.

Mickelson's approach shot to 18 landed above the hole, leaving him about an 18-foot downhill putt for a winning birdie. He got a good read from playing partner Chris DiMarco's putt, then curled in his own putt.

Mickelson leaped for joy while the crowd roared its approval. Mickelson arguably has been the most popular golfer of his generation for his aw-shucks attitude and unending willingness to sign autographs and mingle with the fans.

With a major championship finally under his belt, Mickelson finally was rid of one tag, but quickly got another. "Now we can finally stamp him, 'Approved,'" long-time friend and fellow pro Davis Love III quipped.

Hockey's Lost Season

In just their 12th season in the NHL, the Tampa Bay Lightning won hockey's Stanley Cup championship with a 2–1 victory over the visiting Calgary Flames on June 7. That capped a dramatic, seven-game Stanley Cup Finals series in which each of the last four games was decided by only one goal (one of those games went overtime and another into double overtime).

The exciting series, however, would be the last NHL action for quite some time. That's because several months later, on September 15, the Collective Bargaining Agreement (CBA)—the contract between team owners and the players' union—expired. The next day, NHL owners agreed to lock out the players (that is, to prevent them from practicing, playing, or using team facilities) until a new agreement was in place. (A lockout is different from a strike. In a strike, the employees refuse to work.)

As with previous strikes or lockouts in Major League Baseball and the NFL, money was at the heart of the dispute, with the two sides disagreeing over revenue sharing and a salary cap. Revenue is all money earned by an organization. The owners and the players' union did not ratify a new agreement until July 22, 2005, long after the 2004–05 season should have ended. By February of 2005, the league gave up hope of salvaging any part of the season and canceled it altogether.

The NHL thus earned the sad distinction of being the first major pro sports league in North America to lose an entire season because of a labor dispute.

Motor City Mania

The Detroit Pistons beat the Los Angeles Lakers 100–87 in Game Five of the NBA Finals June 15 in Auburn Hills, Michigan, to win the league championship for the third time overall, but for first time since 1990. It also marked the first NBA championship for Hall-of-Fame head coach Larry Brown.

Brown had coached seven ABA or NBA teams in a highly successful, but well-traveled coaching career before arriving in Detroit in the fall of 2003. He guided the Pistons to 54 regular-season wins and a second-place finish in the Central Division behind a balanced team featuring point guard Chauncey Billups, swingman Richard "Rip" Hamilton, and center Ben Wallace.

In the playoffs, Detroit beat Milwaukee and New Jersey before downing Central Division-champion Indiana in six games in an intense Eastern Conference Finals. In the NBA Finals, the Pistons had little trouble dispatching the Western Conference-champ Lakers four games to one.

The series marked the end of an era for basketball in Los Angeles. The Lakers were back in the Finals for the fourth time in five seasons (they won the championship three years in a row beginning in 2000), but superstars Kobe Bryant and Shaquille O'Neal no longer could coexist on or off the court, while veterans such as forward Karl Malone and guard Gary Payton were nearing the end of their careers.

After the season, Los Angeles parted ways with its hulking center, O'Neal,

2004

whom they traded to Miami for three players and a draft choice. Malone retired, and Payton was traded along with forward Rick Fox to Boston. Even coach Phil Jackson, the architect of the team's three titles in the early 2000s, retired. (He eventually came back for the 2005–06 season.) Only Bryant was left in a major rebuilding effort that brought the Lakers back to the top of the NBA before the end of the decade.

Athens Games

For the first time since the modern Olympic Games began in Athens in 1896, the Summer Olympics returned to the Greek capital. More than 10,000 athletes from 201 countries participated. The United States took home the most medals, earning 36 gold and 102 overall.

The lion's share of the American medals came from swimmer Michael

Basketbrawl

A fight that erupted late in a game between the Indiana Pacers and the Detroit Pistons on November 19 carried over into the stands and left the NBA with a big black eye.

Indiana handily was leading defending-champion Detroit on the Pistons' home court in Auburn Hills, Michigan, when an on-court fight broke out in the final minute of the game. (The Pistons, who beat the Pacers in the Eastern Conference Finals in the spring,

sometimes rubbed opponents the wrong way with their rugged style of play.) Left at that, the incident would only have gone down as a minor skirmish.

But when a cup of soda was thrown at Indiana's Ron Artest in the aftermath of that fight, the Pacers' star broke one of the cardinal rules of sports—he charged into the stands. Teammate Stephen Jackson soon followed him, and the incident quickly dissolved into a chaotic scene of players and fans fighting in the stands and some fans moving onto the court to avoid the altercations.

In the end, Artest was suspended for the rest of the season and Jackson for 30 games. Seven other players from both teams were handed smaller suspensions. Players and fans formally were charged with assault or trespassing.

The fight highlighted the increasing need for security at sports events, which had seen several incidents between players and fans in the 2000s—although none as ugly as this one. It also illustrated the increasing disconnect between many millionaire athletes and the fans that idolize them.

Phelps, who earned six gold medals and eight medals overall. Phelps' four gold medals in individual events equaled American swimmer Mark Spitz' feat at the 1972 Summer Olympics, and his eight overall medals marked the first time anyone had done that except for a Russian gymnast at the 1980 Olympics, which the United States and many other countries boycotted. Even still, Phelps' amazing performance was only a warmup act for his incredible run at the 2008 Olympics in Beijing.

Among the other American highlights at the games, the women's softball team overpowered its opponents on the way to a gold medal, and the women's soccer team beat Brazil 2–1 in extra time in an exciting final to win the gold medal. Gymnast Carly Patterson became only the second American woman to win the all-round gold medal in her sport.

It wasn't all good news for the United States, though. For the first time since NBA players were allowed in the Olympics in 1992, the American men's basketball team lost a game, dropping its opener to Puerto Rico by 19 points. Another loss to Lithuania soon followed, and eventual gold medalist Argentina knocked out the Americans in the semifinals. Still, the United States salvaged a bronze medal by beating Lithuania in a rematch.

A Curse Reversed

"Reverse the Curse," Boston Red Sox' fans implored their team when it became apparent it was headed to another trip to the Major League Baseball postseason—its fifth in the past 10 years.

Fastball from Finch *Star pitcher Jennie Finch led the U.S. women's softball team to a dominating gold-medal performance at the Summer Olympics.*

"The Curse" was the Curse of the Bambino, which started after Boston sold Babe "The Bambino" Ruth to the New York Yankees in 1919. In the years since that event, Boston had not won a single World Series. The Yankees had won 26. But 2004 was different. After many agonizing close calls over the years, the Red Sox finally did it. They won their first World Series since 1918. Boston beat the Cardinals October 27 in St. Louis 3–0 to complete a four-game sweep in the Fall Classic.

Other Milestones of 2004

Birdstone (right) upsets Smarty Jones.

stars with performance-enhancing drugs.) By 2005, all the defendants in the BALCO trial had struck deals with federal prosecutors. Under the agreements, they did not have to reveal the names of any athletes that may have used the illegal drugs.

✔ Former NFL star Pat Tillman, a member of the elite U.S. Army Rangers, was killed while fighting in Afghanistan on April 22. Tillman, 27, played for the Arizona Cardinals from 1998 to 2001 before enlisting in the military in the aftermath of the infamous September 11 terrorist attacks.

✔ After steadfastly refusing to acknowledge that he ever bet on baseball, former Major League star Pete Rose admitted to doing so in his autobiography called *My Prison Without Bars* (Rodale Press, January 2004). Rose admitted to betting on baseball while managing the Cincinnati Reds. He said he sometimes bet on the Reds, but never against them. Major League Baseball, however, did not lift his lifetime ban from the sport.

✔ The Patriots won the Super Bowl for the second time in three seasons, outlasting the Carolina Panthers in a wild fourth quarter to win game XXXVIII in Houston on February 1, 32–29. Adam Vinatieri, who kicked the game-winning field goal in New England's win in Super Bowl XXXVI, did it again, booting the winning 41-yarder with four seconds left.

✔ Baseball's steroids scandal stayed in the headlines when U.S. Attorney General John Ashcroft announced a 42-count indictment February 12 against individuals involved in the Bay Area Laboratory Co-operative scandal. (BALCO allegedly had provided sports

✔ Two weeks after winning the Kentucky Derby on May 1, Smarty Jones took the Preakness Stakes by a record 11 1/2 lengths. The three-year-old's bid for horse racing's coveted Triple Crown ended, however, when 36–1 long shot Birdstone beat him in the Belmont Stakes on June 5 with a strong finishing kick. Smarty Jones, who finished second, retired after that, with just the one loss in nine career races.

✔ The Montreal Expos, Major League Baseball's first Canadian team, played its final season north of the border. The Expos, who began as a National League expansion team in 1969, played 39 seasons in Montreal and reached the postseason only one time (1981). The team moved to Washington, D.C. for the 2005 season and became known as the Nationals.

✔ Mia Hamm, who led the United States to a gold medal at the 2004 Summer Olympics, and who was perhaps the most famous American women's soccer player ever, retired. Hamm had two assists in her last match, a 5–0 victory for the United States over Mexico December 8 in Carson, California.

A big part of the story was how the Red Sox got to the World Series. After winning 98 regular-season games but finishing three games behind the Yankees and earning a wild-card berth in the playoffs, Boston easily dispatched the Anaheim Angels in the A.L. Division Series. In the League Championship Series, though, the Red Sox fell behind the hated Yankees three games to none, and entered the bottom of the ninth inning of Game Four in Boston trailing 4–3.

With their backs to the wall, the Red Sox scratched out the tying run, helped by a key steal from pinch-runner Dave Roberts. In the 12th, slugger David Ortiz won it with a two-run home run.

The next night, Boston rallied from two runs down in the eighth inning to send the game into extra innings. And again, Ortiz delivered the game-winning hit, a single in the 14th inning of a 5–4 victory that sent the Series back to New York.

At Yankee Stadium, the Red Sox jumped out to big leads early in Games Six and Seven and won 4–2 and 10–3 to complete a stunning comeback. Game Six was memorable mostly for the seven strong innings turned in by right-hander Curt Schilling, who pitched with blood seeping through his socks from loosened stitches in his injured ankle. It was the first time that any team in a major sport had come from that far behind

Diamond Gems

Two future members of the National Baseball Hall of Fame pitched landmark games during the 2004 season.

On May 18, the Arizona Diamondbacks' Randy Johnson tossed a perfect game—27 batters faced and 27 batters retired—in a 2–0 victory over the Braves in Atlanta. Johnson struck out 13 batters, including the final hitter (Eddie Perez) on a 98 mile-per-hour fastball. At 40, the 6-foot 10-inch lefty was the oldest player ever to toss a perfect game.

On August 7, at San Francisco's SBC (now AT&T) Park, the Chicago Cubs' Greg Maddux won his 300th career game. The right-handed Maddux overcame a shaky start, got some help from his offense—Corey Patterson and Moises Alou slugged two-run homers—and won 8–4. Maddux was the 22nd Major League pitcher (just the 10th since World War II) to reach that magical milestone. He would go on to pitch through 2008, the season he turned 42, and finish with 355 wins.

(three games to none) to win a playoff series.

The World Series against St. Louis was almost anticlimactic. Boston scored in the first inning of all four games and never trailed at any time. Outfielder Manny Ramirez batted .412 with 1 home run to earn Series MVP honors.

It had been 86 years since their last championship, but Red Sox fans didn't have to wait long for another. Just to prove 2004 was no fluke—and to dispel any lingering doubts that the curse really was a thing of the past—Boston would win the World Series again in 2007 (see page 73).

2005

Patriots Get Their Kicks

For the third time in four seasons, Adam Vinatieri's field goal made the difference as the New England Patriots won the Super Bowl. And while this one wasn't nearly as dramatic as his final-seconds kicks to win Super Bowls XXXVI and XXXVIII, it was no less satisfying. Vinatieri booted a 22-yard field goal midway through the fourth quarter, and the Patriots held on to beat the Philadelphia Eagles 24–21 in game XXXIX in Jacksonville on February 6.

The game was tied at 14–14 early in the fourth quarter before New England took the lead for good with a 66-yard touchdown march. Corey Dillon scored the go-ahead points on a two-yard run with 13:44 left, but it was versatile rushing-receiving threat Kevin Faulk who made the key plays on the drive. Faulk caught screen passes of 13 and 14 yards, and also had 12- and 8-yard runs.

The next time the Patriots had the ball, Vinatieri kicked his field goal for a 24–14 lead, which held up after the Eagles scored a touchdown with 1:48 remaining. Philadelphia got the ball back one more time after that, but New England safety Rodney Harrison intercepted a pass to seal the victory.

Quarterback Tom Brady passed for 236 yards and two touchdowns for New England. Wide receiver Deion Branch earned game MVP honors after tying a Super Bowl record with 11 catches (for 133 yards). Donovan McNabb passed for three touchdowns for the Eagles, but also was intercepted three times.

With the victory, the Patriots joined the Dallas Cowboys of the 1992 to 1995 seasons as the only NFL teams to win the Super Bowl three times in a four-year span.

MLB Goes to Washington

Baseball's steroid scandal remained firmly in the spotlight as a result of several developments in 2005, none bigger than Congressional hearings in Washington, D.C. beginning on March 17.

Even before that, Major League Baseball and the Players' Association agreed on new, tougher punishment guidelines for players using performance-enhancing drugs, including a 10-day suspension for a first positive test. After the 2005 season, the length of the initial suspension was increased to 50 days.

Top of the World *Tim Duncan of the San Antonio Spurs needs both hands to hold the NBA Finals MVP and NBA championship trophies (page 51).*

Commissioner Bud Selig and several current and former players testified about steroid use before the House Committee on Government Reform in March. Unfortunately, the most memorable testimony did not shed baseball in a positive light. Former slugger Mark McGwire insisted he was "not there to talk about the past." (McGwire eventually admitted to using performance-enhancing drugs, but not until 2010, after

2005

he was hired as a hitting coach by his former team, the St. Louis Cardinals.)

Dominican native Sammy Sosa, whose home-run race with McGwire captivated the nation in 1998, skirted several questions, claiming that he didn't understand them well enough, while the Baltimore Orioles' Rafael Palmeiro steadfastly said that he never took performance-enhancing drugs. That testimony appeared ludicrous when Palmeiro was suspended for 10 days August 1 for testing positive.

After completing his suspension, the 40-year-old Palmeiro went 2-for-26 in seven games before announcing his retirement.

Major Quest

Before he even turned 30 late in the calendar year in 2005, Tiger Woods already had accomplished just about everything there is to accomplish in golf—the biggest amateur events, dozens of professional championships, multiple PGA money titles and Player of the Year awards, and undisputed status as the No. 1-ranked golfer in the world. He has made little secret of his ultimate career goal, however: passing Jack Nicklaus' hallowed record of 18 major golf championships. (The men's golf majors include the Masters, the U.S. Open, the British Open, and the PGA Championship.) Woods took a major step closer toward that objective when he won the Masters and the U.S. Open in 2005.

At the Masters at Augusta (Georgia) National Golf Club beginning April 7, Woods won in part by pulling off one of the most memorable shots in PGA history during the final round. Locked in a tight duel with playing partner Chris DiMarco, Woods missed the green with his tee shot at the par-three 16th hole. His subsequent chip appeared, at first glance, to be way off target. But Woods intentionally chipped above and well left of the pin to let the slope of the green carry the

On the Hot Seat *Baseball superstar Sammy Sosa faced tough questions about the use of performance-enhancing drugs in his sport. His evasive, unspecific answers did not go over well with fans or the media.*

Hurricane Relief

As often happens in the wake of tragedy, people from all walks of life—including the ultra-competitive world of sports—came together to help victims of Hurricane Katrina, which hit the coast of Louisiana and neighboring states on August 29. The most destructive hurricane ever to hit the United States killed at least 1,600 people and caused more than $75 billion in damage.

Individuals, teams, and leagues all pitched in to the relief effort. Athletes such as brother quarterbacks Eli and Peyton Manning, natives of New Orleans, donated their time and money to the cause. The NFL's New Orleans Saints established a Relief Fund that raised more than $1 million to help local causes.

The NHL had players wear special jerseys on opening night in the fall, jerseys that were then auctioned to raise money for relief efforts. The list went on and on.

New Orleans was hit especially hard when its levees gave out, and residents flocked to the Louisiana Superdome (the home of the Saints), which served as a major evacuation center. But the Superdome itself suffered damage, and the Saints spent the 2005 season playing their home games at the Alamodome in San Antonio, Texas, and at Tiger Stadium in Baton Rouge, Louisiana. The Saints did not return to a refurbished Superdome until an emotional Monday-night victory over the Atlanta Falcons early in the 2006 season.

---

ball toward the hole. The ball rolled and rolled until it came to the lip of the cup, stopped for a tantalizing instant, and then fell into the hole. "In your life, have you ever seen anything like that!" announcer Verne Lundquist famously proclaimed to the CBS television audience. The shot gave Woods a two-stroke lead, and he eventually won the tournament on the first hole of a sudden-death playoff with DiMarco.

Woods didn't need such dramatics at the British Open beginning July 14 at The Old Course at St. Andrews in Scotland. He led wire-to-wire and finished five strokes ahead of second-place Colin Montgomerie.

Woods' victories pushed his career total to 10 major championships and vaulted him into third place on the all-time list, behind only Nicklaus and Walter Hagen (11). By decade's end, Woods was up to 14 major titles.

The Quiet Champs

On the list of famous National Basketball Association champions, it's easy to overlook the San Antonio Spurs. Alongside the Boston Celtics' and the Los Angeles Lakers' lengthy list of championships, the Spurs' two titles (entering the 2004–05 season) hardly seemed worth noting. Plus, the Spurs generally have been a team devoid of nationally known players—and devoid of the big egos that sometimes accompany stardom.

NBA championships are all the recognition San Antonio needs, though, and in the 2004–05 season, the Spurs won it all for the second time in three years. (They would make it three titles in five seasons by winning again in 2006–07.)

Led by forward-center Tim Duncan and guards Tony Parker and Manu Ginobili, San Antonio went 59–23 during the regular season to win the inaugural

End of an Era

Jerry Rice, generally considered the greatest wide receiver in NFL history and arguably the greatest player ever, retired shortly before the 2005 season began. He decided against playing a 21st NFL season.

Rice entered the league as the 16th overall pick of the 1985 draft by the San Francisco 49ers. He played his first 16 seasons in San Francisco before finishing his career with three-plus seasons in Oakland and part of his final year in Seattle. He made the Pro Bowl 13 times, was a first-team All-Pro choice 10 times, and was inducted into the Pro Football Hall of Fame in his first year of eligibility in 2010. His final career totals were staggering: 1,549 catches for 22,895 yards and 197 touchdowns, with 207 touchdowns in all. Those are all NFL records, and none figure to be broken for a long time.

As a kicker to his accomplishments, Rice also achieved an unusual feat his final season, when he played in 17 games during the 16-game schedule in 2005. That's because after six games he was traded from Oakland, which had not had its bye week yet, to Seattle, which still had 11 games to play.

Southwest Division championship in the newly realigned NBA. In the playoffs, the Spurs breezed to victories over the Denver Nuggets, Seattle SuperSonics, and Phoenix Suns to reach the NBA Finals.

Defending-champion Detroit provided a tougher test in the Finals, and the series went the full seven games. In the finale, on June 23 in San Antonio, Duncan scored 25 points and grabbed 11 rebounds in the Spurs' 81–74 victory. He was named the Finals MVP.

By the end of the decade, the Spurs had quietly established themselves as the NBA's most consistent winner of the first 10 years of the new millennium. They posted an average of 58 victories during the regular season, made the playoffs all 10 seasons, and won three league championships (to go along with another title won in 1999).

Mr. Versatility

NASCAR's Tony Stewart is one of those drivers who will get behind the wheel of anything, anywhere, anytime. Before he joined NASCAR full-time in 1999, he'd won championships in Karts, Sprint Cars, Midgets, and Indy Cars. By 2002, he added a NASCAR season title to that list.

So when NASCAR instituted a new playoff format called the Chase for the Sprint Cup in 2004 (it's called the Chase for the Nextel Cup now after a sponsor change), that wasn't going to faze the driver in the recognizable orange Home Depot No. 20 car. Stewart finished sixth overall in the first Chase in 2004, in which only the top 10 (now it's the top

Tony the Tiger *Versatile and talented NASCAR driver Tony Stewart dominated the 2005 season, with 17 top-five finishes helping him claim his second season championship.*

12) drivers can compete for the title over the final 10 races of the season, with the points reset.

In 2005, Stewart was NASCAR's dominant driver. He finished in the top 10 in 25 of 36 races, including a stretch of 13 in a row, and had 17 top 5 finishes. He won five of those times in a seven-race stretch in the summer that vaulted him to the top of the standings. And he won on tracks as varied as the long track at Daytona, the short track at New Hampshire, and the road courses at Sonoma (California) and Watkins Glen (New York).

Fittingly, Stewart became the first—and, so far, only—driver to win NASCAR championships under the season points format and the Chase playoff format.

Seventh Heaven

Even before Lance Armstrong stood on the victory podium on the Champs-Élysées in Paris on July 24, he knew it was time. On the verge of his record seventh Tour de France championship—all of them coming in a row since 1999—he knew it was time to step down and give someone else a chance at the yellow leader's jersey. "There's no reason to continue," he said. "It's time for a new face, a new story. No regrets."

2005

Armstrong's 2005 victory in cycling's biggest competition had been a foregone conclusion for a while. He won in record time, and finished 4 minutes and 40 seconds ahead of his nearest rival, Italian cyclist Ivan Basso.

Number seven, then, was perhaps the easiest of all of Armstrong's victories. The only pressure came from knowing—at least at the time—that it was his last Tour de France (although he later came out of retirement to race again in 2009; see page 85).

"I wanted to go out on top," he said. "That was the only pressure."

Fourth-and-9

Down by three points and nine yards from a first down, No. 1-ranked USC had one shot to hold onto its top ranking. However, the Trojans converted that key play late in the fourth quarter of a 34–31 victory over the Notre Dame Fighting Irish in South Bend, Indiana, on October 15 to extend its school-record winning streak to 28 games.

Notre Dame had taken a 31–28 lead with 2:04 remaining on quarterback Brady Quinn's five-yard touchdown run before the Trojans took over for one last possession beginning at their 25-yard line. On fourth-and-nine from the 26, quarterback Matt Leinart audibled to a pass to Dwayne Jarrett. The wide receiver caught the ball in stride and raced 61 yards to the Irish 13-yard line.

Five plays later—after officials had to clear the field of fans who thought the game ended in a Notre Dame victory on the previous play when the clock operator didn't realize a fumbled ball had gone out of bounds—Leinart sneaked over from the one-yard line with three seconds left to give USC the victory.

Big Catch *USC's Dwayne Jarrett sprints away from Notre Dame defender Ambrose Wooden on a dramatic 61-yard reception late in the fourth quarter that set up the Trojans' winning TD.*

Sox of a Different Color

One season after the Boston Red Sox ended an 86-year championship drought, the American League's Chicago

Other Milestones of 2005

✔ The University of Southern California Trojans (USC) thumped the Oklahoma Sooners 55–19 in a matchup of 12–0 teams in the BCS National Championship Game at the Orange Bowl in Miami on January 4. Still, the arguments continued: unbeatens Auburn and Utah felt they deserved a chance at the Trojans in the title game.

✔ The North Carolina Tar Heels scored the game's final five points to beat the Illinois Illini 75–70 in the NCAA Men's Basketball Tournament final on April 4 in St. Louis. It was the fourth national title for North Carolina. Illinois equaled an NCAA record by winning 37 games (against only two losses), including a thrilling 90–89

North Carolina

victory over Arizona in the Midwest Region final to reach the Final Four.

✔ After the lost season of 2004–05, the NHL returned to the ice with all 30 teams in action on October 5. The Ottawa Senators beat the Toronto Maple Leafs 3–2 on opening night to become the first team to win under the league's new overtime shootout rule. (Games still tied after five minutes of overtime go to a three-man shootout to determine the winner.)

✔ After a one-year retirement, nine-time NBA-championship coach Phil Jackson returned to the Los Angeles Lakers' bench for the 2005–06 season.

White Sox ended their own 88-year championshipless streak by sweeping the National League-champion Houston Astros in four games in the World Series. The final game was a 1–0 victory at Houston on October 26. Four White Sox pitchers combined to shut down the high-scoring Astros on five hits, with Bobby Jenks getting his second save of the Series.

The key game, though, came the night before at Minute Maid Park. Houston, needing a victory after dropping the first two games in Chicago, jumped out to a 4–0 lead through four innings. But the White Sox rallied with five runs in the

fifth, and the game eventually went to the ninth inning tied at 5–5. The Astros left the bases loaded in the bottom of the ninth, then stranded two aboard in the 10th and 11th innings. In the top of the 14th, former Astro Geoff Blum broke the tie with a solo home run, and Chicago went on to win 7–5.

The tight contest was similar to the entire Series. Although a sweep appears lopsided on the surface, the White Sox won their four games by a combined total of only six runs. That equaled a 55-year-old big-league record for the smallest run differential in a World Series sweep.

2006

In-Vince-ible

The 2006 Rose Bowl, which also served as college football's national championship game, had everything a fan could want: a perfect setting, a pair of unbeaten teams in Texas and USC—who were also the nation's two highest-scoring squads—the two most recent Heisman Trophy winners (quarterback Matt Leinart and tailback Reggie Bush, both of USC), and the two players who had finished one-two in the season's Heisman race (Bush and Texas quarterback Vince Young). Whew!

USC strutted into Pasadena for the January 4 game boasting a 34-game win streak. The Longhorns countered with a 19-game win streak of their own. Both teams put up about 50 points per game.

The game itself was mesmerizing. Leading 38–33 with 2:13 remaining in the fourth quarter, the Trojans went for it on fourth-and-two from the Longhorns' 45-yard line. Bush, though healthy, was not on the field. The Longhorns stuffed Trojan running back LenDale White.

On the ensuing drive, Texas faced a fourth-and-five from the eight-yard line with less than 30 seconds remain-ing. Young, who had already scored two touchdowns, took a shotgun snap. His receivers covered, the 6-foot 5-inch quar-terback won a footrace to the right pylon to score the winning touchdown and se-cure Texas its first national championship since 1970. Many experts immediately called it one of the best games in college football history.

Grand Torino?

The world converged on the north-ern Italian city of Torino (or Turin) for the XX Winter Olympic Games. Every Olympics provides a rich tapestry of win-ners and losers, and heroes and villains. Certainly, these Games fit that model.

Touchdown . . . Title *Texas QB Vince Young dives for the first of his two TDs in the BCS Championship Game.*

The American team seemed more steeped in characters than character at the outset of the Games. Alpine skier Bode Miller, the reigning World Cup champion, claimed that Olympic medals did not mean much to him. Speed skaters Shani Davis and Chad Headrick seemed more intent on undermining each other than on beating anyone skating under a different flag. And the biggest showoff in the group was a male figure skater, Johnny Weir, who missed his bus and then claimed that he'd left his "aura" back at the Olympic Village.

Miller, an overwhelming favorite, failed to win a medal but reportedly had plenty of fun away from the slopes. Weir also missed out on a medal while figure-skater Michelle Kwan, the most renowned talent on the American squad, pulled a groin muscle and dropped out of the Games before her competition began. For Kwan, a five-time world champion, it marked her third Olympics in which she failed to win gold.

The moment that put the American team in the worst light, however, came in the hottest new Olympic event, snowboard cross. In the gold-medal race, Lindsey Jacobellis had a seemingly insurmountable three-second lead over Tanja Frieden of Switzerland heading into

2006

the next-to-last jump. But this was snowboarding, so Jacobellis, 20, chose to reach back and grab the tail of her board—a maneuver known to snowboarders as a method grab—on the jump to showboat for the spectators.

Red = Gold *Flame-haired snowboard superstar Shaun White was a star at the Torino Olympics, winning the half-pipe competition with stunning moves. His youthful joy cemented his status as a rising star in action sports.*

Jacobellis fell on the landing. In a classic tortoise-versus-hare finish, Frieden blew past Jacobellis for gold while the American settled for silver. "Snowboarding is fun," Jacobellis would say in her defense. "I was having fun."

Nobody was having more fun than fellow snowboarder Shaun White. The free-spirited, flame-haired White (aka, "The Flying Tomato") was as refreshing as the Alpine air as he shredded his way to gold in the men's half-pipe. Shani Davis, a speed skater, made history in becoming the first black person to win an individual gold medal in a winter Olympic event (the 1,000 meters). Apolo Anton Ohno, with a cool soul-patch beard to go with his cool name, also took home a gold and two bronzes in short-track speed skating. And lightly regarded Julie Mancuso, who had never won a World Cup race, won gold in the giant slalom.

No athlete in red, white, and blue, though, did more to restore American pride than speed skater Joey Cheek. While the feud between teammates Davis and Headrick raged on at the Oval Lingotto, Cheek earned a gold medal in the 500 meters and a silver medal in the 1,000 meters. The United States Olympic Committee (USOC) handed out bonuses of $25,000 and $15,000, respectively, for those medals, but Cheek donated his winnings to Right to Play, an international humanitarian organization founded by former Olympic gold medalist Johann Olav Koss of Norway.

In an era, and at an event, too far given over to selfish behavior, Cheek's gesture was the fuel that sustained the Olympic flame.

Cinderella Wore Green

When George Mason, a team from the lightly regarded Colonial Athletic Association (CAA) earned an invitation to the NCAA men's basketball tournament (also known as "March Madness" or "The Big Dance"), critics in the basketball media howled. After all, the Patriots had failed even to win the CAA championship.

The Patriots were given a No. 11 seed and little chance to advance beyond an opening-round game with Michigan State. The Spartans, after all, had won the national championship in 2000. George Mason surprised the Spartans, but struggled in the opening moments of their second-round contest against North Carolina. The Tar Heels, the defending national champions, led 16–2 early in the game.

The Patriots, who took their cue from their fun-loving coach, Jim Larranaga, battled back and shocked the heavily favored Tar Heels with a 65–60 victory. That was followed by a defeat of fellow Cinderella mid-major Wichita State. That victory set up a date with No. 1-seed Connecticut, the third opponent Larranaga's no-names would face that had already won a national championship earlier in the decade.

The top-ranked Huskies led by nine points at halftime. In the second half, though, the Patriots were fearless. Despite yielding an average of three to four inches per man, the Patriots would out-rebound Connecticut by a 37–34 margin.

The Patriots actually led 74–70 in the closing moments, but the Huskies fought back to send the game into overtime. In the huddle before the extra period began, Larranaga told his players that there was no place he'd rather be, and no people he would rather be with at that moment. Duly inspired, George Mason went out and won in overtime, 86–84.

In the Final Four the following Saturday, George Mason lost to eventual national-champions Florida and the Cinderella story was over. Few would deny, though, that more fans recall the run that George Mason made in the tourney—beating three former national champions from the past six years—than that the Gators won it all.

Oh, Behave

As was the case for most of the decade, athletes made too many negative headlines.

In March, *San Francisco Chronicle* reporters Mark Fainaru-Wada and Lance Williams released the book *Game of Shadows*, the culmination of their two-year investigation into the alleged use of steroids by Barry Bonds. The San Francisco Giants outfielder was on the verge of breaking the all-time home run record. The evidence detailed in the book showed that other prominent Major League Baseball players, not only Bonds, were involved. The book marked a turning point in baseball's stance on performance-enhancing drugs.

In May, American sprinter Justin Gatlin tied track and field's world record for the 100 meters, at 9.77 seconds. Then he tested positive for a banned substance and was banned from competition for eight years (a sentence that was later commuted to four). His 9.77 performance was also annulled.

In July, American cyclist Floyd Landis stormed back in the final stages to win the Tour de France. Landis, however, tested at almost three times the legal ratio of testosterone to epitestosterone. In September, Landis was disqualified. The title was awarded to Spaniard Oscar Pereiro.

Not Just Americans

Cyclist Floyd Landis' apparent doping skullduggery (see page 59) was not the most abominable act to take place on European soil in the summer of 2006. The World Cup, staged in Germany, had an all-European final pitting France against Italy. In the seventh minute, Zinedine Zidane, the greatest footballer in French annals, scored to put France ahead 1–0. Zidane had already won the Golden Ball award as the top player of this World Cup and that goal, his third in a World Cup final, tied him for the most all-time.

Italy tied the score in regulation. Then, in extra time, Zidane and Italian defender Marco Materazzi got into a heated war of words. The Frenchman lost his composure. With hundreds of millions watching around the world, Zidane got a running start and head-butted Materazzi in the chest. For that, he received a red card and in this, his final match, was kicked out of the game.

Italy won the final on penalty kicks while one of the greatest soccer players of all-time exited on the sourest of notes.

Win Some, Lose Some

On April 9, Phil Mickelson won the prestigious Masters golf tournament at the Augusta (Georgia) National Golf Club for his second consecutive championship in a major—he won the final major of the 2005 season at the PGA Championship in August—and for his third career major title. That was the good news for the popular golfer from San Diego, California. The bad news? Mickelson had a third consecutive major championship in his grasp on June 18 at the U.S. Open at Winged Foot Golf Club in Mamaroneck, New York, before a stunning final-hole collapse handed the title to Australian Geoff Ogilvy.

At the Masters, Mickelson outlasted not only his fellow competitors, but also the elements in a two-shot victory over South Africa's Tim Clark. Mickelson was four shots behind leader Chad Campbell entering the third round on Saturday, which is "moving day," in golf parlance. Mickelson made his move with a two-under-par 70 that day, while many others on the leaderboard, including Campbell (who shot a three-over-par 75) struggled in rainy and windy conditions. Thunderstorms eventually suspended play, but Mickelson picked up where he left off by carding a three-under-par 69 in the final round to win his second green jacket as the Masters champion.

At the U.S. Open, Mickelson entered the 72nd, and final, hole with a one-shot lead over Ogilvy before pushing his tee shot on the par-four well left into the trees. Instead of punching out of the trees and playing for an almost certain bogey, which would have meant an 18-hole playoff the next day, Mickelson went for the green, clipped a tree, and barely advanced the ball. His next shot missed the green, and it took him three more shots to get the ball in the hole. His double-bogey left him tied for second place, one shot behind Ogilvy.

It was a bitter defeat for Mickelson, who always dreamed of winning the U.S. Open, and he berated himself afterward for not playing it safe. "I just can't believe that I did that," he said. "I am such an idiot."

Ironically, Mickelson's final-hole disaster only further endeared him to many golf fans, who long have reveled in his go-for-broke style. Fans equally have cheered the affable lefty's many successes and agonized over his spectacular defeats.

Saga of Barbaro

Twenty-six years. Horse racing's Triple Crown—the Kentucky Derby, Preakness Stakes and Belmont Stakes—had never endured such a drought. Beginning with Sir Barton in 1919, there had been 11 Triple Crown winners. However, no three year-old thoroughbred had done so since Affirmed in 1978.

Barbaro should have ended that drought. The bay colt entered the Kentucky Derby, also known as the "Run for the Roses," having won all five of his races. At Churchill Downs, Barbaro won by 6 1/2 lengths even though his jockey, Edgar Prado, never used a whip. That was the largest margin of victory in the Derby since 1946.

Two weeks later, on May 20 at the Preakness, Barbaro was an overwhelming favorite. As he passed the grandstand shortly after the start, the horse pulled up lame. His right hind leg was broken in 20 places, the foot dangling grotesquely. That moment marked the end of his career, and the start of a nationwide infatuation with Barbaro and an obsession with saving the lame colt's life.

Barbaro was transferred to a veterinary facility in Pennsylvania, where he underwent surgery and the type of round-the-clock care normally reserved for heads of state or celebrities. Thousands upon thousands of "Get Well" cards poured in, including one that measured 7 feet by 72 feet. Updates on his condition transcended the sports pages.

Barbaro developed a disease in his hoof known as laminitis, common among four-legged animals. After several surges and setbacks in his recovery, Barbaro was put to sleep in January of 2007, eight months after first pulling up lame. He was cremated, and his remains, as well as a statue, are located outside the entrance of Churchill Downs.

Tiger, Down and Up

Tiger Woods dealt with mortality and proved he was mortal himself in 2006, but by year's end he reasserted himself as the most dominant athlete of the decade.

Get Well Soon *The great champion horse Barbaro was popular among racing fans. When he was injured in the Preakness, thousands sent in "get well" cards like this one.*

2006

On May 3, Earl Woods, Tiger's father, died after a long bout with prostate cancer. Earl was both Tiger's father and his mentor, the man who had taught him to play golf as soon as he could stand on two feet. The two had always been inseparable, on or off a golf course.

Woods, who had finished in a tie for third place at the Masters a few weeks earlier, took a nine-week hiatus. He re-emerged at the U.S. Open at Winged Foot but shockingly missed the cut. It marked the first time in Woods' career, a span of 40 majors, that he had failed to advance to the weekend.

If grief had led to distraction and poor play, failure was the ideal antidote for the 30-year-old. Woods won the final two major championships of the year, the British Open and the PGA Championship, shooting 18 under par in both. At the former, at Royal Liverpool Golf Club in England, Woods won by two strokes.

Four weeks later, beginning August 17, Woods was dominant at the PGA Championship at Medinah, Illinois. In winning his 12th career major, Woods carded only three bogeys, tying a record for the fewest in a major. That same month, he won his 50th career event on the PGA Tour—the Buick Open—to become, at 30 years and seven months, the youngest golfer ever to do so. Woods would win his final six PGA Tour events of the year and won eight events overall.

Dancing Emmitt

Former Dallas Cowboys superstar Emmitt Smith, the NFL's all-time leading rusher, already had a host of trophies and awards from his playing days, including Super Bowl rings, the Pete Rozelle Trophy as the Super Bowl MVP, and an Associated Press award as the NFL's MVP. To his roomful of impressive hardware, he added an unlikely award on November 15: the Mirror Ball Trophy, presented to the winner of television's *Dancing With the Stars* competition.

Dancing With the Stars is a reality TV series in which a dozen or so celebrities

Another Kind of Trophy *NFL Hall of Famer Emmitt Smith showed that he could win away from the field. He and partner Cheryl Burke won TV's* Dancing With the Stars.

Other Milestones of 2006

✔ Kobe Bryant scored 81 points for the Los Angeles Lakers in a 122–104 victory over the Toronto Raptors on January 22. Bryant's 81 was the second-highest points total in one game in NBA history after Wilt Chamberlain's 100-point game in 1962.

✔ Ben Roethlisberger, just 23 years of age, became the youngest quarterback to lead a team to Super Bowl triumph when the Pittsburgh Steelers beat the Seattle Seahawks 21–10 in Super Bowl XL in Detroit on February 5.

Ichiro Suzuki

✔ Japan, led by outfielder Ichiro Suzuki, won the inaugural World Baseball Classic in March. The United States finished with three wins in six games and bowed out in the second round of the 16-nation tournament.

✔ On May 28, San Francisco Giants outfielder Barry Bonds hit his 715th career home run. Bonds' blast, off the Colorado Rockies Byung-Hyun Kim, broke a tie with the legendary Babe Ruth and lifted him into second place on baseball's all-time list, behind only Henry Aaron.

✔ The NHL saw its future as virtuoso talents Alexander Ovechkin (Washington Capitals), 20, and Sidney Crosby (Pittsburgh Penguins), 18, both debuted in the 2005–06 season. Ovechkin, the Russian son of a professional soccer-playing dad and an Olympic basketball gold-medalist mom, won the Calder Trophy as the league's outstanding rookie. Crosby became the youngest player in NHL history to score 100 points in a season.

✔ On November 17, on the eve of "The Game" between the Ohio State Buckeyes and the Michigan Wolverines, legendary retired Michigan football coach Glenn "Bo" Schembechler suffered a fatal heart attack. Ohio State and Michigan were both 11–0 and were ranked one-two in the country entering the annual rivalry game in Columbus, Ohio. The Buckeyes prevailed 42–39.

✔ New York Yankees pitcher Cory Lidle, a licensed pilot, crashed his small plane into a high-rise apartment building on New York City's Upper East Side. Lidle and his co-pilot and flight instructor, Tyler Stanger, died in the crash. Other notable deaths included Boston Celtics patriarch Red Auerbach, golfer Byron Nelson, former heavyweight boxing champ Floyd Patterson, and two-time Olympic decathlon gold medalist Bob Mathias.

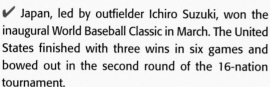

are each paired with one professional dancer. Every week, the couples perform ballroom dance routines, to be judged by a panel of experts and voted on by the television audience. One by one, the teams are eliminated until a champion remains.

In the fall of 2006, Smith was paired with professional dancer Cheryl Burke on the third season of *Dancing With the Stars*.

After nine weeks of competition, the pair reached the finals against actor Mario Lopez and his partner, Karina Smirnoff. Both teams were nearly perfect on the judges' scorecards in the final, but Smith and Burke emerged from the complicated scoring system as the winners.

Four years after he left the NFL, Smith proved he still had winning moves.

2007

Bad News Everywhere

If 2007 was not the worst year in sports, a nadir on and off the fields of play, then it certainly was in contention for such a label. The mishaps and misery began just two hours into New Year's Day with the drive-by-shooting murder of Denver Broncos cornerback Darrent Williams. Only 12 hours earlier, Williams had played in the Broncos' season-ending 26–23 loss to the San Francisco 49ers. As Williams, 24, and friends were driving away from a New Year's Eve party hosted by Denver Nuggets player Kenyon Martin, he was shot once in the neck, killing him instantly.

Williams' murder was a tragedy. It was also foreshadowing for the worst sports year of this decade, if not every other, a year in which the famous were never more infamous. Don't say we didn't warn you.

The bad news continued in February. During the NBA All-Star Game weekend in Las Vegas, NFL cornerback Adam "Pac-man" Jones was at the center of a fight at an adult club. He helped start things by tossing money in the air in the crowded club. In the ensuing chaos, gunshots were fired. Three people were hit, including a security guard who was left paralyzed from the waist down from his wounds. In April, NFL commissioner Roger Goodell suspended Jones for the entire 2007 season, a sanction not assessed a player (outside of drug-related issues) by the NFL in 44 years.

College Football Upsets

If only all sports contests could be even half as thrilling as the Fiesta Bowl battle waged between Boise State and Oklahoma on January 1, 2007. The undefeated Broncos, only the second non-Bowl Championship Series school ever to play in a BCS bowl, shocked the Big 12 champions with a 43–42 overtime win that bested any script Hollywood could hope to write.

Three touchdowns were scored in the final 1:26 of regulation. The Broncos converted a fourth-and-18 from midfield via a hook-and-lateral play to tie the score with just 0:07 left. In overtime Adrian Peterson of the Sooners scored on a 25-yard run—the final carry of his brief, but brilliant, college career—but Boise State replied with another fourth-down

The Right Stuff *Venus Williams showed she still had her winning stroke when she won Wimbledon (page 67).*

conversion for a touchdown, this via a halfback pass.

Then, instead of kicking an extra point to send the game into a second overtime, Boise State won it on a Statue of Liberty play handoff from quarterback Jared Zabransky to tailback Ian Johnson. Instead of spiking the ball in celebration,

Johnson got on one knee to propose to his girlfriend, cheerleader Chrissy Popadics.

Seriously.

The Broncos had only been 7 1/2-point underdogs, though. When the '07 season opened the following September, Appalachian State, a Football Championship Subdivision (FCS; formerly known

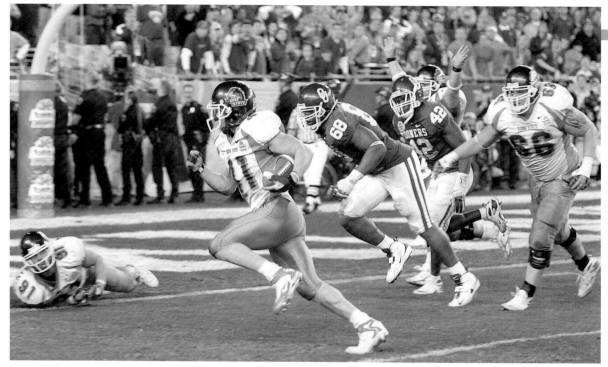

What a Game! *Using a play seen more often on playgrounds than in top-level college football, Boise State upset Oklahoma in one of the most entertaining games of the decade in any sport.*

as Division I-AA) school, was a 27-point underdog at Michigan.

The Wolverines boasted a No. 5 ranking, the all-time most wins in Football Bowl Subdivision (FBS) history, the following spring's No. 1 overall NFL draft pick in offensive tackle Jake Long, and the Big House, its stadium that overflowed with 110,000 rabid fans.

No matter. The Mountaineers, who had won 14 straight games before arriving in Ann Arbor, won 34–31. It marked the first time an FCS/I-AA school had ever beaten a ranked FBS/I-A school, and it easily would have been the year's most monumental upset if not for . . .

. . . Stanford 24, USC 23. In October, the unranked Cardinal entered Los Angeles Coliseum, where the Trojans had won 35 consecutive home games, as 41-point underdogs. Playing inspired football under first-year head coach Jim Harbaugh, Stanford mounted a late drive behind quarterback Tavita Pritchard, who was making his first-ever start (Pritchard had only attempted three passes in his career beforehand). On fourth-and-goal from the USC 10-yard line, Pritchard connected with Mark Bradford on a fade route for the winning score and the greatest upset, based on the point spread, that college football has ever seen.

Beckham Beckoned

David Beckham, the most iconic figure in soccer, if not all of sport globally, signed in January with the Los

Angeles Galaxy of the MLS. Beckham, whose wife Victoria (aka Posh Spice) is nearly as famous as he, left Spain's Real Madrid for a five-year, $250 million contract with the Galaxy and the faint hope of one day being able to say that he helped make soccer as popular as the big three sports in the United States.

As Beckham was welcomed to great fanfare in front of a big crowd, the move made headlines around the world. Few sports figures in this era were as well-known, in and out of the sports pages, as Beckham. For him to leave soccer-mad Europe to come to America, where soccer is a second-class citizen, was a big gamble for him and for MLS. Most of his money, in fact, was based on sales of soccer gear, not on salary for playing. It was a bold move by the Galaxy and MLS to try to help the 13-year-old league take a big jump ahead.

"In my career, I've played for two of the biggest clubs in the world and for my country, and I've always looked for challenges," said Beckham. "While my family is most important, the second biggest thing in my life is the football, I mean the soccer. I'll get used to saying that! But this is a big challenge. Potentially in the States, soccer could be as big as it is around the world. I'm very proud to be part of that."

A similar experiment in 1975 in the North American Soccer League had brought world superstar Péle to the New York Cosmos. That lasted only three years, however. By 2009, Beckham was antsy again, spending part of the MLS season "on loan" to Italian club AC Milan. He did play in Los Angeles often enough to help the team make the 2009 MLS Cup, though they lost there on penalty kicks.

Venus and Serena Return to Form

The Williams sisters, Venus and Serena, opted to take tennis seriously again in 2007. That was bad news for the rest of the WTA Tour.

In January, Serena, 25, journeyed Down Under to play in the Australian Open. Injuries and apathy had taken their toll on the younger Williams sibling the past two years. Though she had seven Grand Slam singles championships to her name, Serena was ranked 81st in the world and went unseeded in Melbourne.

It barely mattered, as Serena crushed top-seeded Maria Sharapova 6–1, 6–2 in the final.

Five months later at Wimbledon, older sister Venus, who also had seven Grand Slam singles titles to her credit at the time, was seeded 23rd at the All-England Club. Despite some early hiccups—Venus was one game away from defeat in each of her first two matches—she won her final four matches in straight sets to win the championship, her fourth at Wimbledon.

In doing so, Venus Williams became the lowest-seeded Wimbledon champion in history. That was almost as impressive a feat as that of Serena, who became only the second unseeded woman in the Open era to win a Grand Slam.

Super Colts

For the better part of a decade, the Indianapolis Colts had been good—but not quite good enough to reach the top of the NFL landscape. In the seven

2007

regular seasons from 1999 through 2005, the Colts reached the postseason six times, only to lose in the AFC playoffs each time. Finally, after winning its fourth consecutive AFC South Division title in the 2006 season, Indianapolis carried its success through the postseason, and the Colts beat the Chicago Bears 29–17 in Super Bowl XLI at Dolphin Stadium in South Florida on February 4. It was the franchise's first Super Bowl victory since the Colts, then in Baltimore, beat the Dallas Cowboys in game V following the 1970 season.

The seeds for Indianapolis' championship were sown in the spring of 1998, when the team selected Tennessee quarterback Peyton Manning with the top overall pick of the annual NFL draft. Manning became an immediate starter for the Colts and, after a 3–13 baptism in 1998, engineered an amazing turnaround

that had the upstart Colts in the playoffs by 1999.

That year, Manning passed for more than 4,000 yards for the first of six years in a row, and earned the first of 10 Pro Bowl selections in 11 seasons through 2009. In 2004, he set an NFL record (since broken) by passing for 49 touchdowns. By 2006, all that was missing was a Super Bowl championship.

In the AFC title game, the Colts beat the New England Patriots, their playoff nemeses and Super Bowl winners three times in the 2000s, 38–24 as Manning passed for 389 yards and a touchdown. Then, in the Super Bowl, Manning earned game MVP honors after passing for 247 yards and a touchdown. Indianapolis fell behind early when the Bears' Devin Hester returned the opening kickoff 92 yards for a touchdown, but dominated play much of the rest of the way.

Spy Games

Eric Mangini made his coaching debut with the New York Jets on September 9 against the team for whom he had formerly worked as an assistant, the New England Patriots. The Jets lost, 38–14. The following day, Mangini accused the Patriots of having videotaped New York's defensive signals from a sideline location during the game. The Jets had confiscated the video camera used by Patriots assistant Matt Estrella during the game.

The NFL would fine the Patriots $250,000 and force them to forfeit their first-round pick in the 2008 NFL draft. New England coach Bill Belichick was fined a heftier sum of $500,000. Belichick also learned a lesson about double-crossing a former assistant who knows the intricacies of one's operation.

Why was videotaping against the rules? It was not a problem if a team could "steal" such signs during a game; that's why teams often use different signs or decoy signers. However, by taping the signs to be decoded later, the Patriots crossed the line. It was a bigger story because of the star power of the Patriots, too.

Two footnotes, one significant and one trivial, go along with the Colts' victory. Significant: When Indianapolis' Tony Dungy and Chicago's Lovie Smith squared off that day, it marked the first time that the Super Bowl matched two African-American head coaches. Trivial: It was the first time a Super Bowl game ever had been played in the rain.

A Mouth Roars

Don Imus, whose syndicated "Imus in the Morning" radio show was simulcast on MSNBC television, found out just how far you cannot go on the radio. On April 4 (the anniversary of the death of Martin Luther King, Jr., of all days), Imus referred to the Rutgers University women's basketball team in a very offensive way. The evening before, the Scarlet Knights had lost to Tennessee in the women's NCAA basketball championship game.

The dialogue between Imus and his producer, Bernard McGuirk, used inappropriate and racist words to describe the mostly African-American Rutgers team. While Imus probably thought he was just joking around, listeners and other critics were outraged and flooded radio stations with calls and e-mails. The story exploded in the media, and Imus' reputation suffered greatly. Advertisers cut their time on the show, and stations dropped him. Eight days after he made his rude remarks, Imus' show was canceled. Though not directly tied to a sports event or personality, the incident showed how much attention anything related to sports got, especially when controversy was involved.

Milestone Event *With the Vince Lombardi Trophy as their goal, coaches Lovie Smith of the Bears (left) and Tony Dungy of the Colts led their teams into the Super Bowl.*

An Error in Judgment

In June, the FBI contacted the NBA regarding suspicions of wrongdoing by referee Tim Donaghy, a 13-year veteran. Donaghy would soon plead guilty to wire fraud and transmitting wagering information through interstate commerce. In short, Donaghy, a "pathological gambler," admitted to sharing information, as well as wagering on NBA games. Donaghy, in other words, was helping gamblers by his actions during games or by providing them with information he should not have revealed.

2007

NBA commissioner David Stern swiftly labeled Donaghy, who would be sentenced to 15 months in prison, a "rogue, isolated criminal." Yet his indictment opened up questions about the integrity of NBA officials and the games themselves. All those calls—and missed calls—that fans had seen in key moments of playoff games? They wondered if maybe there actually was something more than an honest mistake going on there.

The controversy raged for weeks, as other referees worried that they would be swept up with Donaghy. No others were officially included in the investigation, but the suspicion raised by Donaghy's actions has taken a long time to fade away. Almost nothing harms a sport more than the suspicion of cheating by officials.

Vick Goes to the Dogs

Michael Vick was one of the most dynamic players in the NFL. The first quarterback ever to rush for 1,000 yards in a season, he had signed the richest contract in league history in 2005 when he agreed to a 10-year, $130 million deal with the Atlanta Falcons. In 2007, Vick threw it all away.

In July, Vick was indicted by a federal grand jury for owning and operating Bad Newz Kennels, which bred dogs specifically for fighting. Those that performed poorly were put to death by Vick and his associates, the 19-page indictment alleged.

Public reaction was swift and certain: Vick was a villain. Animal-rights groups demanded further justice, and the case received national attention for weeks. In August, NFL commissioner Roger Goodell suspended Vick indefinitely. The Falcons' dual-threat quarterback would plead guilty to the charges. Four months later, he was sentenced to 23 months in prison.

The fall from grace of such a big star was another piece of bad news for the NFL and the sports world, reeling as they were from ongoing drug investigations and a series of off-field violence. Vick himself took a little while to realize the gravity of his situation, at first stonewalling but then coming clean as he realized his position. After serving his time, he was allowed to return to the NFL, signing with the Eagles as a backup quarterback in 2009.

Solo Act

Hope Solo was unbeatable in goal for the U.S. women's soccer team through the first four games of the Women's World Cup in September. Solo recorded three shutouts as the U.S. advanced to a semifinal match against Brazil.

That is when the coach, Greg Ryan, replaced her with 36 year-old Brianna Scurry (a heroine from the 1998 World Cup and the Olympics). The Brazilians won 4–1. "It was the wrong decision, and I think anybody that knows anything about the game knows that," said Solo. "There's no doubt in my mind I would have made those saves. And the fact of the matter is it's not 2004 anymore."

Ryan was widely criticized for the switch. When his contract expired on the last day of the year, U.S. Soccer made a switch of its own, opting not to extend Ryan's contract.

The move raised a lot of questions. Many said that Solo was wrong to criticize the decision publicly, and that she had broken an unwritten rule by saying that her teammate (Scurry) was not up to the job. Ryan hurt his status with the team by his actions, too, and was punished for it. The interaction of coaches and players, and players' increasing public voice was a big reason that the Solo story made headlines. One footnote: In 2009, Solo was named the player of the year by the U.S. Soccer Association.

Baseball's Dirty Laundry

Throughout the decade of the 2000s, the story of drug use in sports became bigger and bigger. Public and government outcry led to the pro leagues doing more and more to try to investigate and combat the problem. Baseball's answer was to hire former United States Senator George Mitchell to prepare a report for Commissioner Bud Selig. Mitchell took almost two years to complete the job.

In December, the 409-page document, nicknamed The Mitchell Report, came out. It reported the rampant use of anabolic steroids and human growth hormone (HGH) in Major League Baseball. The report named 89 players who were alleged to have used performance-enhancing substances. While those names were supposed to remain confidential, certain high-profile ones (such as Roger Clemens and Andy Pettitte) were later leaked to the media.

A New Home Run Champ?

Earlier in the year, baseball got a dose of positive news, though even it came with baggage. On August 7, Barry Bonds hit a full-count pitch from Mike Bacsik of the Washington Nationals over the right-center field wall in San Francisco. It was Bonds' 756th career home run, breaking Henry Aaron's 33-year-old record. The moment was awkward—neither Aaron nor commissioner Bud Selig witnessed the feat in person—due to the strong, even overwhelming, evidence that Bonds used performance-enhancing drugs for much of the second half of his career. Bonds bowed out at season's end with 762 career home runs.

2007

The report created a firestorm of discussion and anger. For years, fans had seen the evidence of drug use, especially those designed to increase a player's size or performance. There had been isolated incidents of players caught using the stuff. However, the Mitchell Report, for the first time, brought names and details into the public eye. As a result, baseball wound up with a black eye, though some did praise it for at least trying to come clean.

However, for many, it was too little, too late. Critics blasted the players named, including some who had previously and vigorously denied using such substances. Many careers were tainted while hundreds of others not named were called into question. The report started a chain reaction of other revelations, as more and more players were revealed to have tested positive for some of these substances in the previous decade.

Other Milestones of 2007

✔ For the first time, the same two schools (Florida and Ohio State) met to decide the national championship in college football and college basketball in the same calendar year. The Gators defeated the Buckeyes in each sport.

✔ At the U.S. Men's Olympic Marathon Trials in New York November 3, Ryan Shay collapsed just past the 5 1/2-mile mark. One of the premier U.S. marathoners of the decade, Shay suffered a massive heart attack due to an enlarged heart condition and died instantly. Most of his fellow competitors, including the winner, Ryan Hall, had no idea what had happened to Shay until they crossed the finish line.

✔ On September 13, the New York Mets were 83–62 and in first place in the National League East by seven games. New York proceeded to lose 12 of its final 17 games, including 6 of its final 7, to miss the playoffs. The epic collapse was punctuated by an 8–1 loss at

Jimmie Johnson

Shea Stadium on the final day of the season to the last-place Florida Marlins. With a win, the Mets would have made the postseason.

✔ As stunning as the collapse of the Mets was the revival of the Colorado Rockies. Colorado won 13 of its last 14 games, including a one-game showdown with the San Diego Padres, to earn a wild-card berth in the postseason. Then the Rockies won all seven of their games in the N.L. playoffs before losing to the Red Sox in the World Series.

✔ Jimmie Johnson repeated as NASCAR's Nextel Cup champion.

✔ Deaths: NFL All-Pro safety Sean Taylor, 24, died of a gunshot wound while confronting burglars in the middle of the night in his home. Also passing: baseball's Phil Rizzuto, football's Bill Walsh, and college football coaching legend Eddie Robinson.

Finally, Some Good News

You might have guessed that when the Boston-based movie *The Departed* won four Oscars, including Best Picture and Best Director (Martin Scorsese), it was going to be a banner year for Boston. The Red Sox swept the Colorado Rockies four games to none in the World Series in October. It was the Red Sox's second championship in the decade. In the 2000s, the Sox would go 8–0 in World Series games.

Meanwhile, in Foxboro, the New England Patriots became the first NFL team to finish a regular season 16–0. While the 1972 Miami Dolphins had also gone undefeated in the regular season (and postseason), the league played a 14-game schedule back then. Sure, there was that nasty little matter of SpyGate in the season opener against the New York Jets, but the Patriots and their GQ-caliber quarterback, Tom Brady, who was only dating one of the world's most beautiful women (supermodel Gisele Bündchen) seemed to enjoy the world's disdain.

Victory was infectious around the Hub. Even the long dormant Celtics, whose last NBA title had come in 1986, were suddenly dominant. Behind the trio of Ray Allen, Kevin Garnett, and Paul Pierce, the parquet predators were an astounding 26–3 on New Year's Eve.

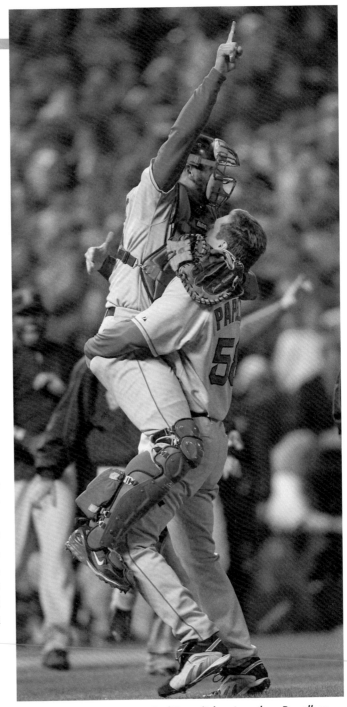

No Curses Here *Boston Red Sox pitcher Jonathan Papelbon lifts catcher Jason Varitek after the Red Sox swept the Colorado Rockies to win their second World Series in four years.*

2008

The Best Year Ever?

If 2008 was not the greatest year ever in sports, it was indeed the cure for the disappointing one that preceded it. From a football stadium in Glendale, Arizona, to a golf course outside San Diego, from a grass-layered tennis court in London to the Bird's Nest in Beijing, witnesses were left in slack-jawed wonder all over the globe.

A few "greatest" nominees from 2008: Super Bowl play (David Tyree's catch), U.S. Open golf finish (Tiger Woods), tennis match (Wimbledon men's final), Olympic performance (Michael Phelps), and Olympic performance lasting less than 10 seconds (Usain Bolt).

America seemed to agree, as television viewers watched in record numbers. Tiger Woods' 18-hole (make that 19-hole) playoff win at the U.S. Open was the most-watched golf event on cable in history. The New York Giants' 17–14 victory over the New England Patriots was the most-watched Super Bowl ever. The Beijing Summer Olympics, the superlative event in this most superlative of years, became the most-watched global event of all time, with 4.7 billion viewers.

Super Game, Super Catch

The New England Patriots entered Super Bowl XLII on February 3 with an 18–0 record. Only the 1972 Miami Dolphins had finished an undefeated season with a Super Bowl triumph, finishing 17–0. The Patriots, behind head coach Bill Belichick and NFL Most Valuable Player QB Tom Brady, had a chance to join them.

Their opponent? The New York Giants, whose quarterback, Eli Manning, was no better than the second-best quarterback (if not third-best, if you consider his dad, Archie) in his own family, behind the Indianapolis Colts' Peyton Manning. The Giants' march to the Super Bowl had been a three-game road trip that included nail-biting victories at Dallas and Green Bay.

New York's last loss, in fact, had been a 38–35 thriller in the regular-season finale to . . . the Patriots. When the two teams met again in Glendale, Arizona, the Giants' fierce pass rush, led by defensive ends Osi Umenyiora and Michael Strahan (playing his final game), harassed Brady all game, sacking him five times.

With 2:42 to play, the Patriots took a 14–10 lead on Brady's six-yard touchdown pass to Randy Moss. On the ensuing drive,

Splish, Splash *When you set a record for Olympic gold medals, you get to shout like Michael Phelps (page 77).*

the Giants faced a third-and-five from their own 44-yard line with 1:15 remaining. That is when Manning and David Tyree, a wide receiver who was primarily a special-teams player, created perhaps the most spectacular play in Super Bowl lore.

Manning, in the pocket, appeared to be in the grasp of Patriots defender Jar- vis Green. Not known for being mobile, Manning eluded Green's clutches, spun away, and heaved a pass 35 yards down the center of the field. Tyree leaped up to make the catch and pinned the football to the crown of his helmet with both hands as safety Rodney Harrison, one of the fiercest hitters in the NFL, strained to

2008

separate the ball from his grasp. All three entities—Tyree, Harrison and the football—landed together with the pigskin still firmly in Tyree's paws.

The reception defied description, if not physics. A few plays later, Manning found Plaxico Burress for the game-winning touchdown pass. The Patriots were denied their perfect season, while David Tyree etched his name into sports history.

No, He Didn't! *Yes, he did! In one of the NFL's most spectacular plays ever, Giants wide receiver David Tyree (85) clutched the football to his helmet and came down with a Super Bowl-saving grab.*

Wounded Tiger Still Dangerous

The U.S. Open, staged at Torrey Pines in San Diego, came down to an 18-hole playoff on June 16 between two men. There was Rocco Mediate, who at 45 looked as if he were barely in good enough shape to take down the storm windows. Mediate, who had six career PGA Tour wins, had to survive a sudden-death playoff just to qualify for the Open.

Then there was the indomitable Tiger Woods, seeking his 14th career major. Mediate himself had described his adversary, who had buried a 12-foot putt on the 72nd hole on Sunday to force the playoff, as a "monster."

Woods took a three-shot lead onto the 11th hole. Mediate, as if writing the plot for the sequel to the golf movie *Tin Cup* (featuring an out-of-nowhere challenger for a major win), stormed back to take a one-shot lead heading into the 18th hole. In fact, he had a 20-foot putt on 18 to win it. Few golfers ever came so close to slaying Tiger.

It was not to be. Mediate missed his putt, while Tiger sank his for birdie. That forced a 19th hole on the playoff—the 91st overall— and Woods took that by one stroke.

"I'm glad I'm done," said Woods, who walked the final 19 holes with a slight limp. "I really don't feel like playing any more."

And who could blame him? It was later revealed that Woods, who had needed pain-killing medicine during the final round, had played with a double stress fracture to his left tibia. He would also shortly need to undergo knee surgery. This, the grittiest win of Woods' career, was also his final tournament of the year.

Beijing

At the outset of the Beijing Summer Olympics, it appeared that everyone's worst fears would be realized. A few days before the Opening Ceremony, a few American cyclists stepped off the plane wearing surgical masks as a precaution against the Chinese city's notoriously polluted air. On the day of the Ceremony itself—8/8/08, since eight is a lucky number in China—as world leaders filed into the Beijing National Stadium (dubbed "The Bird's Nest" for its exterior design), Russia invaded Georgia. Less than 24 hours later, the father-in-law of Hugh McCutcheon, the U.S. men's volleyball team coach, was fatally stabbed at a tourist attraction, the Drum Tower. The assailant, a deranged Chinese man, then leapt to his death.

Then the competitions began. What followed over the next two weeks was instead the realization that we were watching the greatest athletic spectacle of our lifetimes. The highlights:

Michael Phelps

The U.S. swimmer won all eight races that he entered, setting a new gold standard to which all future Olympians must aspire. Performing under the weight of extraordinary expectations, Phelps bested by one Mark Spitz's 36-year-old record for most gold medals (seven) at a single Olympics while also setting seven world records in the process.

Phelps' march to immortality, as dramatic as it was historic, almost ended in his second race. In the 4 x 100 meter relay, anchor Jason Lezak made up a body-length deficit in the final 50 meters against the French world record holder in the event. To do so, Lezak swam the fastest relay leg in history.

After that moment, it was clear that these Games were imbued with a certain magic. In Phelps' seventh race, the 100-meter butterfly, he trailed down to the final stroke, out-touching his Serbian rival by the slightest of margins: one one-hundredth of a second.

Dara Torres

At age 41, Dara Torres was hardly slowing down. In Beijing, the California native became the first American swimmer to compete in five Olympics, and was the first female swimmer above age 40 to participate in an Olympics.

But Torres, whose chiseled body garnered as much attention as her body of work, was there to win. She earned two silver medals in relays. In her final race, the splash-heavy 50-meter freestyle, she lost out on gold by a mere one-hundredth of a second. At another point in her career, Torres might have been crushed, but perhaps knowing how she'd been cheating Father Time for so long, she was able to grin at the irony.

Asked what she was thinking afterward, Torres replied, "I'm thinking I shouldn't have filed my nails last night."

Other American Highlights

More memorable moments from Beijing: The lightly regarded U.S. men's volleyball

Golden Spikes *Clayton Stanley (in red) and the rest of the U.S. men's volleyball team were inspired by the tragic death of their coach's father-in-law early in the Games and rallied to win gold.*

team, which had to deal with the murder of their coach's father-in-law on the opening day of competition, went undefeated to win gold. American shooter Matt Emmons, for the second Olympics in a row, squandered a sure gold medal with a disastrously off-target effort on the last of his 10 shots.

The U.S. men's basketball and women's soccer teams, after disappointing finishes in world competition dating back to 2004, both won gold. Japan stunned the United States in the gold-medal game in softball, ending the Americans' 22-game win streak and denying them a fourth gold in as many Olympics. It would be the final Olympic softball game for at least eight years, as the sport was voted off the 2012 program in large part due to, ironically, American domination.

Lightning Bolt

At any other Olympics, Jamaican sprinter Usain Bolt's trio of world-record dashes would have been the story of the Games. As it was, he still got a lot of well-deserved world attention. In the 100-meter final the 6-foot 5-inch Bolt ran the 100 in a world-record 9.69 seconds despite easing up in the final five to ten meters. After being heavily criticized for "showboating," the aptly named Bolt again electrified the Bird's Nest audience by running the fastest 200 meters in history at 19.30 seconds. No other sprinter had ever set world records in both races at the same Olympics.

As an encore, Bolt ran the third leg for Jamaica in the 4 x 100-meter final, lending an assist to yet another world-record-setting (37.10 seconds) gold-medal performance.

Danica on Top . . . Finally

Danica Patrick won the Indy Japan 300, taking the lead from pole-sitter Helio Castroneves with two laps to go, to become the first female to win an IndyCar race. It was the 50th race of the 26-year-old Patrick's career.

Although Patrick had made inroads in the male-dominated world of auto racing, and even had earned IndyCar's Rookie of the Year award for 2005, she was known mostly for the good looks that landed her numerous endorsement opportunities and in many commercials even before taking any checkered flags.

Patrick's April 20 victory in Motegi, Japan, in the annual IndyCar stop there validated her status as one of the top IndyCar drivers. By year's end, speculation mounted that she also might also one day make the jump to stock cars on the more popular NASCAR circuit.

Of Rays and Rain

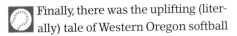

The World Series pitted the Philadelphia Phillies, who had only won one World Series in their previous 125 seasons, and the Tampa Bay Rays, who had never advanced to the postseason in their brief, 10-year history. The Rays were led by American League Rookie of the Year Evan Longoria, while the Phillies had a deep roster led by sluggers Ryan Howard and Chase Utley, as well as Gold Glove fielders in shortstop Jimmy Rollins and center fielder Shane Victorino.

Philly held a three games to one lead in the series when it began raining heavily in the middle of Game Five. Had this occurred in St. Petersburg, Florida, where the Rays' domed stadium is located, the weather would not have mattered. The contest, however, was taking place in Philadelphia.

With the score tied 2–2 in the middle of the sixth inning, the game was suspended—the Rays had tied it on a two-out single moments earlier. It marked the first time a World Series game was not played through to completion or rendered a tie. Rain continued the next day. It was not until two days later, more than 50 hours after the series-clinching game had begun, that the Phillies stormed—excuse the pun—the diamond to celebrate a 4–3 victory and the city's first major sports championship of any kind since 1983.

Heroes of Another Kind

Finally, there was the uplifting (literally) tale of Western Oregon softball

Other Milestones of 2008

✔ On New Year's Day, an NHL-record crowd of 71,217 fans watched the Pittsburgh Penguins play the Buffalo Sabres outdoors—and in a driving snow-storm—in Orchard Park, New York. The "Winter Classic" was decided in an overtime shootout. The Penguins won 2–1 when star Sidney Crosby scored the game-winning goal.

✔ In March, American alpine skier Bode Miller atoned for his abysmal showing at the 2006 Winter Olympics by winning his second World Cup championship in four years. Compatriot Lindsey Vonn, 23, completed the U.S. sweep by winning the women's overall title.

✔ For the first time, all four No. 1 seeds advanced to the Final Four in the men's NCAA basketball tournament. In the final on April 7, Kansas recovered from a nine-point deficit in the final few minutes—thanks to some poor free-throw shooting by Memphis—and forced overtime via Mario Chalmers' three-pointer with two seconds left. The Jayhawks won 75–68 in overtime for their first NCAA title in 20 years.

✔ The Tennessee Lady Vols basketball team beat Stanford 64–48 on April 8 to win its second NCAA championship in as many years and eighth overall under Pat Summitt. A month earlier, the sport's all-time winningest coach (983 victories at season's end) had dislocated her shoulder shooing a raccoon off her back deck.

✔ Belgian tennis star Justine Henin, 25, retired May 14 even though she was the world's No. 1-ranked player at the time. Henin's news came two weeks before the French Open, which she had won four times.

✔ After winning both the Kentucky Derby and Preakness Stakes, 3-10 favorite Big Brown finished in last place in the Belmont Stakes on June 7. Big Brown became the fourth thoroughbred in seven years to win the first two legs of the Triple Crown and then fall short at Belmont.

✔ The Boston Celtics won their NBA-record 17th championship, and first in 22 years, by defeating their old nemesis, the Los Angeles Lakers. The Celtics clinched the title in Boston on June 17 with a 131–92 victory in Game Six. The 39-point margin of victory was the NBA's largest ever in a series-clinching win.

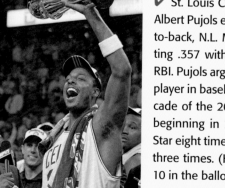

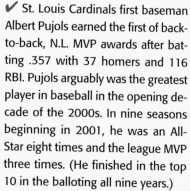

Paul Pierce of the Celtics

✔ St. Louis Cardinals first baseman Albert Pujols earned the first of back-to-back, N.L. MVP awards after batting .357 with 37 homers and 116 RBI. Pujols arguably was the greatest player in baseball in the opening decade of the 2000s. In nine seasons beginning in 2001, he was an All-Star eight times and the league MVP three times. (He finished in the top 10 in the balloting all nine years.)

✔ Annika Sorenstam of Sweden, 38, retired from the LPGA Tour. The dominant golfer of her generation, Sorenstam finished with 72 Tour victories (third all time), including 10 majors.

✔ In December, the Arena Football League suspended operations after 22 seasons of pinball-style, indoor pigskin entertainment.

✔ Manny Pacquiao defeated Oscar De La Hoya December 8 on an eighth-round TKO in a hugely popular welterweight bout.

player Sara Tucholsky. In a playoff game against Central Washington, Tucholsky belted the first home run of her career. As she rounded first base, Tucholsky's knee buckled. She was unable to walk.

College softball rules said that teammates were not allowed to assist Tucholsky. If the coach chose to put in a pinch-runner, the home run would not count and the runner would start on first base. The situation was a tough one for Tucholsky, playing in her final season, and for the Western Oregon coach.

In a display of sportsmanship that would cheer the world, two players from Central Washington moved over to Tucholsky. They put down their mitts and picked up the injured home-run hitter. They then carried her around the bases, making sure she stopped to touch each base. The home run counted and, in fact, it helped Western Oregon beat Central Washington, ending its season, too. The image of the two players carrying their injured opponent showed that amid all the bad and weird stuff that was happening in sports and with athletes that there was still a lot of good that could come from competition.

"In the end, it is not about winning and losing so much," said Mallory Holtman, one of the two players who hoisted Tucholsky. "She hit it over the fence and was in pain, and she deserved a home run."

Now That's Sportpersonship *After she hurt her knee running out a home run, Western Oregon's Sara Tucholsky was carried around the bases . . . by her opponents from Central Washington.*

2009

III for XLIII

One team, the Pittsburgh Steelers, already had five Super Bowl championships, tied for the most ever. The other team, the Arizona Cardinals, hadn't been in a championship game since 1947. Together, these two unlikely opponents put together one of the most entertaining and nail-biting Super Bowls yet.

The game on February 1 was a back-and-forth affair, but Pittsburgh seemed to have the upper hand, thanks to the first of three remarkable plays. The Steelers had gained a 17–7 halftime lead with the longest play in Super Bowl history. Pittsburgh linebacker James Harrison intercepted a pass by Kurt Warner and returned it 100 yards as the first half expired.

However, with three minutes left in the game, the Cardinals took the lead. Star receiver Larry Fitzgerald, who would set NFL postseason records for touchdown catches and receiving yards, teamed up with Warner for a stunning 64-yard score. All of a sudden, the surprising Cardinals had a trophy almost in their grasp.

But Pittsburgh quarterback Ben Roethlisberger got one more chance. He teamed with receiver Santonio Holmes and others to drive the Steelers to the six-yard line. With just 35 seconds left, Holmes made an amazing, fingertip, toe-tapping catch. The Steelers hung on to win 27–23 and capture their record sixth Super Bowl title.

Steroids Scandals Continue

Baseball took two more big hits in the ongoing steroid scandal that had distracted players and fans for most of the decade. In February, news broke that three-time MVP Alex Rodriguez had used steroids during his time with the Texas Rangers. He later admitted that he had let his cousin inject him with what he thought were vitamin supplements starting in 2001 and continuing for two years. "I didn't think they were steroids," Rodriguez said. "That's part of being young and stupid. It was over the counter. It was pretty simple. All these years I never thought I did anything wrong." Few people believed his story, but since he had not tested positive during baseball's annual exams, he faced no punishment from the sport. His personal credibility was deeply

It Was a Brees *Amid flying confetti, Saints quarterback Drew Brees helped cap off the decade of the 2000s with the first Super Bowl win for New Orleans (see page 87).*

hurt, however, as he had adamantly denied using drugs during a television interview in 2007.

Further reports from a 2003 test, which was supposed to be secret, said that David Ortiz, star slugger of the Red Sox, had also tested positive. "Big Papi" denied it, and little came of that story.

A much bigger deal came from one of Ortiz's former Red Sox teammates.

2009

Manny Ramirez, who had joined the Los Angeles Dodgers in 2008, was suspended from baseball for 50 games for testing positive for a banned substance. Ramirez did not test positive for steroids. However, his blood showed levels of a drug used by steroid users to rebuild their testosterone, a drug also used by pregnant women. Ramirez returned later in the season, but, like Rodriguez, his public persona was deeply hurt by the admission.

Perfect . . . Catch

In more than 130 years of Major League Baseball, only 18 pitchers have thrown a perfect game. But none of them got as much amazing last-inning help as Mark Buehrle of the Chicago White Sox. On July 23, the left-hander was mowing down the Tampa Bay Rays. He allowed no baserunners of any kind through eight innings and was three outs away from baseball history when Gabe Kapler drove a ball to deep center field.

Center fielder Dewayne Wise was off with the crack of the bat. He jumped at the wall and reached up to snag the ball just before it left the ballpark. As he fell to the ground, the ball popped out of his glove, but Wise grabbed it with his other hand to record the out.

The miraculous catch preserved Buehrle's "perfecto," and he got the final

A Huge Soccer Upset

The U.S. national soccer team rarely dominates the American sports scene, but their success at the Confederations Cup in June earned them well-deserved attention. In a semifinal match, the United States defeated Spain, which was ranked number one in the world at the time, for one of the biggest wins in American soccer history. Young forward Jozy Altidore scored early and veteran Clint Dempsey added a clincher late in the game to cap the upset. In the final game of that tournament, the United States led Brazil 2-0 at halftime. However, the mighty Brazilians stormed back to win 3–2. It was a disappointment, but still a great inspiration for the Yanks.

Later in the summer, the U.S. team qualified for its fifth straight World Cup, to be held in South Africa in June 2010.

two outs to add his name to the record book . . . with a little help from a friend.

Armstrong Returns

After winning seven Tour de France bicycle races while also overcoming cancer and becoming an international legend, Lance Armstrong retired from racing in 2005 (see page 53). However, he missed the action, so he came back this year to try again. And he almost added another page to his legend. Armstrong was among the leaders in the race, and in fact wore the leader's yellow jersey for a while. But in the tough mountain stages, Spain's Alberto Contador pulled away to ruin Armstrong's comeback chances. Still, the American did finish third, proving that he still had a lot of gas in the tank . . . even on a bike.

Lightning Strikes Twice

Speaking of leaving gas in the tank: While Jamaican runner Usain Bolt had stunned the world at the 2008 Olympics, winning gold and setting world records, many felt that he still had more to give. He had pulled up slightly in the finals in Beijing, so could he actually post a better time?

The answer was yes, as Bolt proved at the World Track & Field Championships in Berlin in August. The speedster blazed through the 100 meters in 9.58 seconds, shaving 1/10 of a second off his world record. If you think that's not that much time, consider that no one had lowered it by that much in one race in more than 88 years.

He proved to be more than a one-race wonder when he also set a new world record in the 200 meters, at an almost-frightening 19.19 seconds. Bolt has set almost unapproachable standards in the sprint races, but who's to say that his own lightning won't strike again.

U.S. sprinter Tyson Gay set a new American record at 9.71 seconds in that 100-meter race in Berlin, but it was little comfort as he watched Bolt's breathtaking performance ahead of him.

Serena Blows a Gasket

Tennis stars have been known to have emotional outbursts, often in frustration at a missed shot or anger at a blown call. Broken rackets, yelling, pointing, and more are not unknown. In fact, the sport has a system for penalizing players who go too far with such tantrums. At the 2009 U.S. Open, that system, and one star player, got the headlines.

Serena Williams, for more than a decade one of the top players in the world and the 2009 Wimbledon champion, was trailing late in a semifinal match against Kim Clijsters at the U.S. Open in New York City. After Williams made a serve, the back-line judge called her for a foot fault. This very rare foul means that a player stepped on the back line during her serve. Williams went ballistic, screaming and yelling and pointing her racket at the official. The umpire, who is the head official, warned Williams and then awarded her opponent a penalty point. Bad news for Williams, for that penalty point was enough to give the game, set, and match to Clijsters.

2009

The angry tirade damaged Williams's otherwise fine reputation. She was fined more than $80,000 and put on probation for two years. Another such screaming fit and she'll lose more than just a match—it could mean a suspension.

Godzilla Strikes! *Yankees slugger Hideki Matsui, known to his fans back home in Japan as Godzilla, was named the World Series MVP after hitting .615, including this key homer in Game 2.*

Yanks Back on Top

In 1923, Yankee Stadium opened, and the New York Yankees brought home a World Series championship. In 2009, a new Yankee Stadium opened . . . and history repeated itself. The Yankees won their 27th World Series title, more than twice as many as any other team, by defeating the Philadelphia Phillies in six games. The Yanks' championship total is the highest of any pro team in North American sports, ahead of the Montreal Canadiens' 24 Stanley Cups and the Boston Celtics' 17 NBA crowns.

The Yankees were led by a few of the players on whom they lavished more than $400 million in contracts before the season. Pitcher C.C. Sabathia won his start in the Series, while first baseman Mark Teixiera slugged and played great defense. Star third baseman Alex Rodriguez finally shook off a career-long postseason slump and had six homers in the playoffs and World Series combined. In the World Series, Hideki Matsui became the first designated hitter (and first Japanese player) to be named MVP, thanks mostly to his record-tying six RBI in the clinching game.

Four for J.J.

NASCAR has been going around in circles—really, really fast—for more than 50 years, but it has never seen a champion like Jimmie Johnson. He became the first driver ever to win four straight championships when he roared to victory in the Chase for the Nextel Cup in 2009. Johnson continued the consistent, steady success that he has had since his career started in 2001. In fact, he has not finished lower than fifth in any season since 2002. In winning his fourth straight title (topping former record-holder Cale Yarborough, who won three titles in a row beginning in 1976), Johnson won seven races, including three in the playoff-like, 10-race Chase that ends the season.

Johnson's total of four career championships ties him with Jeff Gordon, who actually is a co-owner of Johnson's car and his teammate at Hendrick Motorsports. Both of those drivers are still chasing the all-time record of seven career titles won by Richard "The King" Petty and Dale Earnhardt Sr.

Nearly Perfect Football

The New Orleans Saints were once so bad that fans wore paper bags over their heads at games and the team was known as the "Aints." But like New Orleans itself, rising out of the disaster that was Hurricane Katrina, the Saints showed in 2009 that anything is possible.

The Saints won their first 13 games of the season, with QB Drew Brees heading up a powerful offense. They scored 35 or more points in six of their victories, then whomped Arizona 45–14 in the first round of the playoffs. In the NFC Championship Game, kicker Garrett Hartley sent the Saints to their first Super Bowl with a 40-yard field goal in overtime.

Meanwhile, the Indianapolis Colts were on a pretty hot streak, too. Led by Peyton Manning, who won his record fourth NFL MVP, Indianapolis went 14–2 and faced little trouble in the playoffs.

Athletes on Twitter

Celebrities of all stripes jumped on Twitter in 2009, and sports stars were no exceptions. One web site counted more than 1,100 pro and college stars with Twitter accounts, letting their fans in on just about anything that crossed their minds . . . or their keyboards. NBA star Shaquille O'Neal claimed the most numbers of followers among athletes, with more than 2.6 million readers as of the end of 2009, while cycling hero Lance Armstrong was read by 2.2 million.

Bengals receiver Chad Ochocinco became well-known for his "tweets," some of which tweaked NFL officials. Some players in college and the pros actually got in trouble for things they wrote. Running back Larry Johnson of the Chiefs criticized his coach and used inappropriate language in some tweets and actually ended up being let go by the team.

While using Twitter to connect with fans was a positive for many athletes, others were learning that sometimes TMI—too much information!—can be a dangerous thing.

These two hot-streak teams met in Super Bowl XLIV in Miami in February 2010. The Saints offense was on full display, with Brees going 32-for-39 and throwing two touchdown passes. However, it was a big defensive play that cemented the victory for New Orleans. Terry Porter intercepted a pass by Manning and returned it 74 yards for a clinching score in their 31–17 win. The entire city of New Orleans celebrated, pouring out onto the streets to dance and sing. It was the end of a long road for a team that had been playing since 1967 without any sort of title.

For the Colts, even with the loss, the season capped off a record-setting decade. Their 116 wins in the 2000s were the most in any single decade in NFL history. Their 23 consecutive wins over 2008-09

2009

also set a new mark, topping the Patriots' 21 straight in 2002-03. The other big NFL story of 2009 was the second un-retirement for Brett Favre. The NFL's all-time leader in just about every passing statistic had left his longtime team, the Packers, after 2007, only to re-emerge as a New York Jet in 2008. After again "retiring," he was lured out by the Vikings in 2009 and led them to the NFC Central title.

The Last Smile? *Tiger Woods again dominated golf in 2009, winning the FedEx Cup and six other tournaments. By the end of the year, however, his life had taken an ugly turn.*

Tiger Trouble

The final year of the decade came to a bumpy end for the most famous athlete in the world. Golfer Tiger Woods had made positive headlines earlier in 2009 when he bounced back from knee surgery to return to the top of his sport. Though he didn't win any majors, he did capture titles in six other events.

His whole world changed in early December. Very early one morning, word flashed around the world that Tiger had been "seriously injured" in a car accident in front of his Florida home. The first word was that he had been taken to the hospital after his wife had smashed a window to drag him from the car. That report generated sympathy, until details emerged that changed the picture entirely.

Yes, there had been an accident, and yes, Tiger had suffered some minor cuts and bruises. However, his ensuing silence about the event opened up the floodgates of speculation. With no news from Tiger, gossip web sites and bloggers filled the empty space with guesses. Was Tiger fleeing from a fight with his wife? Had they been arguing about whether he had been with other women? Was he under the influence of prescription drugs when he crashed? No one had answers to those questions, and Tiger's reputation crashed. He asked for privacy while he and his family dealt with what he thought was a private matter, but he had not counted on the worldwide fascination with celebrity. For years, he had worked carefully to create a perfect image. With the smash of a fender on a fire hydrant and his evasive answers, that image was smashed.

Other Milestones of 2009

✔ The women's basketball team from the University of Connecticut didn't lose a game all season, going 39–0. It was the third time the school has gone undefeated, and the sixth time it won the NCAA basketball championship.

✔ Everything old was new again at the British Open. At the age of 59, golfing legend Tom Watson came within one stroke of winning the legendary tournament, thrilling fans around the world. Watson, who lost to Stewart Cink in a playoff, had won five British Opens earlier in his career.

✔ In one of the biggest upsets in horse-racing history, 50–1 longshot Mine That Bird won the Kentucky Derby. The horse later won the Preakness Stakes before coming up short in the Belmont Stakes.

Sidney Crosby

✔ Superstar guard Kobe Bryant led the Los Angeles Lakers to their 15th NBA championship. The Lakers defeated the Orlando Magic in five games, and Bryant was named the Finals MVP.

✔ Hockey fans got their wish, as the game's two top stars faced off in the Stanley Cup Finals. In the end, Sidney Crosby's Pittsburgh Penguins overcame Alexander Ovechkin's Washington Capitals to win the Cup.

✔ The New Jersey Nets set a new NBA record for futility. They lost their first 18 games of the 2009–10 season before defeating the Charlotte Bobcats in December. The Miami Heat and Los Angeles Clippers held the old record of 17 straight Ls to start a season. New Jersey ended the season with an NBA-low 12 victories.

As the year was ending, Tiger revealed the truth: He had indeed been unfaithful to his wife. On December 11, he announced that he was taking time off from golf. "After much soul searching, I have decided to take an indefinite break from professional golf. I need to focus my attention on being a better husband, father, and person," Tiger wrote on his Web site.

While Tiger and his family began dealing with the fallout from his bad choices, his decision to step away from the golf course put enormous pressure on the PGA Tour. The entire sport had almost completely depended on Tiger for more than a decade; sure enough, fan interest and television ratings were down early in the 2010 season (at least until Tiger returned to play his first tournament of the new year at the prestigious Masters in April).

Still, the news wasn't all bad: A host of young players stepped to the fore and proved that golf's future was still bright. Among them: the United States' Anthony Kim, Northern Ireland's Rory McIlroy, and Colombia's Camilo Villegas.

RESOURCES

2000s Events and Personalities

The 2000s (American Popular Culture Through History)
By Bob Batchelor (Westport, Connecticut: Greenwood Press, 2008).
Check out the key people, places, and things of the opening decade of the 2000s, from youth issues to advertising, fashion, music, and lots more.

Lance Armstrong: A Biography
By Bill Gutman (New York: Simon Pulse, 2009).
A top writer of sports books for young readers looks at the ongoing saga of one of the greatest athletes of the era. He covers Armstrong's battles with both cancer and fellow riders.

For the Love of the Boston Red Sox
By Saul Wisnia (New York: Publications International, Ltd., 2009).
A veteran sportswriter tells the story of the Red Sox colorful history—including, of course, the team's World Series championships in the 2000s—through anecdotes, trivia, photos, and more.

Venus and Serena Williams: A Biography
By Jacqueline Edmondson (Westport, Connecticut: Greenwood Press, 2005).
Part of the Greenwood Biographies Series, the author tells the life stories of tennis' most famous siblings.

American Sports History

The Complete Book of the Olympics
By David Wallechinsky and Jaime Loucky (London: Aurum Press, 2008)
An extremely detailed look at every Winter and Summer Olympics from 1896 to the present, including complete lists of medal winners and short biographies of important American and international athletes.

The Encyclopedia of North American Sports History, Second Edition
By Ralph Hickok (New York: Facts on File, 2002)
This title includes articles on the origins of all the major sports as well as capsule biographies of key figures.

Encyclopedia of Women and Sport in America
Edited by Carol Oglesby et al. (Phoenix: Oryx Press, 1998)
A large overview of not only key female personalities on and off the playing field, but a look at issues surrounding women and sports.

Encyclopedia of World Sport
Edited by David Levinson and Karen Christensen (New York: Oxford University Press, 1999)
This wide-ranging book contains short articles on an enormous variety of sports, personalities, events, and issues, most of which have some connection to American sports history. This is a great starting point for additional research.

The ESPN Baseball Encyclopedia
Edited by Gary Gillette and Pete Palmer (New York: Sterling, 2008, fifth edition)
This is the latest version of a long-running baseball record and stats books, including the career totals of every Major Leaguer. Essays in the book cover baseball history, team history, overviews of baseball in other countries, and articles about the role of women and minorities in the game.

ESPN SportsCentury
Edited by Michael McCambridge (New York: Hyperion, 1999)
Created to commemorate the 20th century in sports, this book features essays by well-known sportswriters as well as commentary by popular ESPN broadcasters. Each decade's chapter features an in-depth story about the key event of that time period.

NFL Record & Fact Book
Edited by Jon Zimmer, Randall Liu, and Matt Marini (New York: Time Inc. Home Entertainment, 2010)
An indispensable reference source for NFL fans and media personnel.

The Sporting News Chronicle of 20th Century Sports
By Ron Smith (New York: BDD/Mallard Press, 1992)
A good single-volume history of key sports events. They are presented as if written right after the event, thus giving the text a "you are there" feel.

Sports of the Times
By David Fischer and William Taafe. (New York: Times Books, 2003)
A unique format tracks the top sports events on each day of the calendar year. Find out the biggest event for every day from January 1 to December 31.

Sports History Web Sites

ESPN.com
www.sports.espn.go.com
The Web site run by the national cable sports channel contains numerous history sections within each sport. This one for baseball is the largest and includes constantly updated statistics on baseball.

Official League Web Sites
www.nfl.com
www.nba.com
www.mlb.com
www.nhl.com
Each of the major sports leagues has history sections on their official Web sites.

Official Olympics Web Site
http://www.olympic.org/uk/games/index_uk.asp
Complete history of the Olympic Games, presented by the International Olympic Committee.

The Sports Illustrated Vault
http://sportsillustrated.cnn.com/vault/
Since its first issue in 1954, Sports Illustrated *has been a must-read for fans everywhere. You can go down memory lane in this trove of features, photos, and covers from the magazine.*

Sports Reference
www.sports-reference.com
By far the most detailed central site, including separate sections on baseball, basketball, football, hockey, and the Olympics. The sections include player stats, team histories, records from all seasons past, and much more.

INDEX